Muslim Female Education
Veil to Moon

Muslim Female Education

Veil to Moon

Rahat Abrar

Reference Press

New Delhi-110 002

Muslim Female Education
Veil to Moon

ISBN: 978-81-8405-081-3

₹ 700/-

First Published 2014

Published by:
Reference Press
4831/24, Ansari Road,
Darya Ganj,
New Delhi-110 002.
INDIA
Phones: 23260807, 41563444
Fax: 41563334
E-mail: info@essessreference.com
www.essessreference.com

Cover Design by *Patch Creative Unit*

Printed and bound in India at Salasar Imaging Systems.

Dedicated to:

My Parents

(Late) Israrul Haq Siddiqui

(Late) Yaseen Fatima

and

My Family

Shamim Asmat (wife), Talha Israr (son), Subia Rahat (daughter) and Haris Kamal (son in law).

Contents

Preface

Education in general and female education in particular, is a vital subject. Education for Muslims and more emphatically, education for Muslim girls and women holds further significance. Muslim female education, in a special manner, has been in focus, for debate, for a good time. Contrary to common perception, Islam makes it mandatory for its followers to seek knowledge and even travel to distant lands, in search of it. Holy Quran says that the Almighty has given us knowledge and skill to grab it and impart it to others also. Quranic commands are enthusiastic to provide the people — men and women — with such knowledge, so that they may be able to make distinction, between good and evil and emerge out, successfully shaping their life, in a better way. Islam showers on its followers, varied ideas and knowledge, in terms of education. It teaches them a substantial lesson, regarding morality of masses.

Islam has a modern outlook for education. It lays emphasis on enriching a child, with education. For this purpose, Islam holds parents, teachers, rulers and the government, equally liable to take the responsibility to provide useful and better education to children — male and female. Islam talks about a specific budget and allocation of funds, for education and also calls for a perfect assessment system. In Islam, for imparting education, the role of parents has been defined well, with a belief that a child learns his first lesson from his mother only.

Islam makes the attainment of education foremost, in its agenda, but, ironically, its followers — the Muslims or at least a large section of the community — have been ignoring its importance and significance. Islam does believe in gender equality also. It has bestowed equal rights to women, in all walks of life. But, in practice, some members of the Muslim community, have been ignoring or at least sidelining the interests of their better half — women. However, things have changed over the years.

The movement of Female Muslim education is more than a century old now. The Muslim girls are not only obtaining higher education in all disciplines, but they have proved to be the best achievers. They are scaling new heights, True to the sense of the words, they have come a long way, from behind the *Hijab* (veil) to *Mahetaab* (moon), they have covered a long and fruitful journey. Now, perhaps, even sky is not the limit, for them.

This study, based on years long research and a hectic academic exercise, encompasses all aspects and dimensions of Female Muslim Education, right from the birth of the movement to the present day. Hopefully, it would be able to stir the calm waters and at least create some anxiety, among thinkers, scholars and educationists, regarding the subject and bring a sort of awareness in the society at large. The author is bound to be grateful to all those, who would bother to go through this modest work and take pains to enlighten him, with their thoughtful remarks.

—Author

Acknowledgement

I feel privileged to pay my sincere thanks and regards to all those, without whose help, I might not have been able to accomplish this tough job. I extend my heartfelt gratitude to Prof. Athar Siddiqui, the eminent scientist; Mr. Shakeel Ahmad Khan, former Librarian; Mr. Mehr Ilahi of GEC, AMU, and Mr. Azeemuddin, the great grandson of Maulvi Nizamuddin Husain, proprietor of Nizami Press, Badaun.

I also feel indebted to Prof. Shan Muhammad, former Director, Sir Syed Academy; Prof. A.R. Kidwai, Director, UGC Academic Staff College; Prof. Shafey Kidwai, H.O.D., Depatt. of Mass Communication, AMU and Prof. Farhat Hasan, Department of History, University of Delhi, for their valuable suggestions.

And above all, I am greatly thankful to my old friend Dr. Muzaffar Husain Syed, Head, Academic Research Bureau, New Delhi, without whose support and cooperation, this project would not have finally been shaped and the book could not have seen the light of the day. His keen interest in getting the book, edited by one of his associates and aiding in typing and proof reading the book, in an error free manner, contributed a lot to this endeavour of mine.

I am also duly thankful to Mr. Sumit Sethi, the Publisher of this book, who took pains to get it printed and published, in a very short time.

— (Dr.) Rahat Abrar

1

Introduction

It is common knowledge that the position of women in India is worse than their counterparts, in most other places in the world. The position of Muslim women is no better, and as studies by Zoya Hasan and Ritu Menon have shown, one area, in which they lag behind men, as also women of other religious communities, is access to education. Some scholars attribute this to their faith and others to the 'veil'.

Present work, in a way contests these positions and highlights the history of women's education in India. In fact, even if the picture appears bleak today, it has nothing to do with either their faith or culture, for, in the past, when women were making rapid strides in education, they had all these even then. This study explores the development of women's education, and highlights the courage, strength and optimism of the reformers and their work, and also reveals the immense obstacles, against which, Muslim women's education developed in India.

Once, India came under colonial rule, with the growing influence of utilitarianism on state policies, traditional educational system was replaced with the modern European system of education. In 1837 English was declared to be the official language, replacing Persian. State patronage to traditional learning came to an end, and the British government, in its search for English educated clerks forced the Indians to take to English language and modern (Western) learning.

The Muslims generally refrained from Modern education, considering it to be un-Islamic, but what did definitely push them against English was the bitter experience of ruthless massacres, by the British in the wake of the suppression of the revolt of 1857. A memorandum signed by eight thousand Muslim *Ulema* was given to the Governor-General in this regard. Muslim intellectuals were divided into two camps. In one camp, were the traditionalists, opposing English education and modern values, while, in the other, were the reformers, who considered modern education necessary for the advancement of Muslims in India.

Sir Syed Ahmad Khan was the typical representative of the second group and vigorously advocated the cause of modern education for Indian Muslims. Education was very close to the heart of Sir Syed and he relentlessly strove for educational uplift of his fellow countrymen. He tried to correlate science with religion. He had a deep insight into history of nations. He knew that Muslims had attained glory, as long as they were engaged in scientific studies and research. The cause of their decline was their departure from rational enquiry to science (which is one of the obligatory injunctions of the Holy Quran). Loss of rational outlook led the Muslims to confine their women to the household chores, denying them access to education.

One of the great men of his time, Sir Syed came forward with his mission of educational uplift of the Muslim community. For this purpose, women's cooperation was a prerequisite. He knew that he would not succeed, unless he moulded the minds of women, educated them and changed their traditional outlook. He wanted to bring them at par with men. His first lecture which he delivered from the platform of the 'Scientific Society' focused on the marriage of widows. He wrote extensively on women's education and expressed his views, in his editorials and columns.

He vehemently argued the case of female education, as a national necessity. In an article, published in *Institute Gazette*, he mentioned that 'our argument in favour of the education of our women is the desirability of rendering them, as suitable companions and helpmates to ourselves'.

Sir Syed was the first Muslim thinker of the nineteenth century, who sought to strike at the roots of age-old gender bias. He maintained that civilized countries clamoured a lot for the gender equity. He discussed rights of women in his periodicals, time and again, emancipation and empowerment of women also appeared to have drawn his attention.

Deputy Nazeer Ahmad was one of his companions, who contributed a lot, towards moulding the minds of the people in this direction. He wrote many novels, centred on the theme of women's education. Similarly, Khwaja Altaf Husain Hali pleaded, forcefully, the cause of women's education, through his writings and even asserted, "O' my mothers, sisters and daughters ...the destiny of nation rests with you." Hali opined: "No nation can progress without women's education. If they are left behind, in the field of education, Muslims will never be able to progress in the true sense of the word. It is inhuman and barbarous to deprive women of their right to education."

Hakeem Faseehuddin, popularly known as Ranj Merathi, wrote a book, namely, *Tazkirah Baharistan-e-Naaz,* in 1864, before the birth of Aligarh movement, in which he made, a particular mention of women's education. Ranj Merathi was in fact a harbinger of change in society, and advocated strongly for social awareness, among women. It was a period, when women's education was considered to be a taboo, and they were confined to household chores. Two more imprints of the *Tazkirah* appeared in 1869 and 1882. And in 1878, Durga Prasad Nadir came up with *Chaman Andaz,* followed by *Shameem-e-Sukhan* in 1882, by Maulvi Abdul Hayi (known as Safa Badauni). By that time, the number of Urdu poetesses had grown up to 151. One thing which was common to all the works, was the promotion of women's education.

Apart from poetry, Urdu journalism, too, helped in bringing consciousness, among women, and to create a conducive environment, for the spread of women's education. Women's magazines and periodicals were launched for the first time, towards the end of 19th century. *Rafeeq-e-Niswan* was the first magazine for women, published in 1880, from Lucknow. Then came *Akhbar-un-Nisa* (1884; Delhi), *Muallim-e-Niswan* (1886; Hyderabad), and *Tahzeeb-e-Niswan* (1898; Lahore). Shaikh Muhammad Abdullah, who had got training, under Sir Syed, published a magazine, *Khatoon* in 1904 from Aligarh.

Soon, a society, composed of broad minded and educated Muslims and influenced by the movement, launched by Sir Syed Ahmad Khan came into being. They supported the cause of women's education, with great enthusiasm.

Soon after the first generation of Muhammadan Anglo-Oriental (MAO) College had finished education, a pressing need was felt for the education of women. These people provided a renewed vigour to the cause of women's emancipation and equal rights for them. In the meantime, Shaikh Abdullah started a girls' school at Aligarh. All his friends made valuable contributions. But, he had to bear the brunt of scathing criticism, because the majority of Muslim population was against women's education. He was ruthlessly denied the permission to carry on his activities, anywhere on the campus of MAO College. Even the Principal, Mr. Archbold considered girls' school as an ill omen for the education of boys. Owing to these bottlenecks, the girls' school was started in Tantan Para, an old locality, about five kilometre from the MAO College campus. Later on, when the currents of resistance subsided, it was shifted to Marris Road. Today, it is one of the key institutions for women in the country. A century ago, Muslim lady teachers were rare to find, and so male teachers were hired to teach girls, from behind a curtain. Today, of course, the scenario has totally transformed. Former students of this institution are doctors, engineers, lawyers, scientists, politicians, space scientists and what not! In fact, there is hardly any discipline of life, in which students of this college have not gained recognition.

The last two decades of the 20th Century registered a wave of awareness, with regard to education, among Muslims. As far as, the girls are concerned, they have come out of their houses and are eager to gain higher education. Kindled with the fire of emancipation, their hearts throb to go beyond the sky. The long cherished dream of self-reliance has come true, through education. Women at Aligarh are achieving remarkable goals today. At a previous Annual Convocation, at the Aligarh Muslim University, an unassuming girl, clad in *Hijab*, Dr. Sumaiya received as many as twelve medals in the prestigious course of medicine and surgery. Her feat indicated that Muslim girls were advancing in the field of education. Another engineering graduate from the Aligarh Muslim University, Khushboo Mirza, played a leading role in the launch of Chandrayan, the first ever Indian satellite, sent to the moon.

Truly speaking, depriving women of education is contrary to the teachings of Holy Quran and Traditions of the Prophet (Pbuh). So, now education of women is a part and parcel of Muslim society. Even Muslim Ulema, who were once opposed to girls' education, are running schools for girls. Their syllabi have carefully been formulated, in order to empower them to secure their rights. Apart from computer education, there are various other professional packages for them. The purpose is to make them prosper in life and enable them to refute authentically, any charges labelled against Islam. Besides religious education, there are many institutes, for providing girls with modern education. They have excelled boys in many ways. In academic as well as vocational spheres, the ratio of girls goes in an upward direction, as compared to boys.

Present work is a tribute to Shaikh Muhammad Abdullah, for his extraordinary services in the cause of women education. His dream, envisioned, over a hundred years ago, has now come true.

2

Sir Syed and Women's Education

Sir Syed Ahmad Khan (1817-1898) was one of the greatest social reformers in modern India. He was one of those early pioneers who recognized the critical role of education for the empowerment of the poor and backward Muslim community. He contributed much to the development of the modern society of the subcontinent. He established the Mohammadan Anglo Oriental College in 1877 at Aligarh as the first effort to take the reluctant and obstinate Muslim community towards modern education in India. He regards education alone as a means for national progress. If education is sufficiently spread in Muslim community, it will take us out of the present morass of decline.

Aligarh movement was launched by Sir Syed as a positive action; which was to be the fountain head of all educational and cultural programmes which led their bearing upon Muslims in particular and national cultural life in general in the last quarter of nineteenth century.

Going through the life of Sir Syed Ahmad Khan, one comes across two significant events, which brought about a sea change in his life. One was the 1857 revolt, mistakenly known as 'Mutiny' and another was the historic visit of Londan between 1869-70, he envisaged education as a means of opening the window on the west.

He was so depressed by the events of 1857 that he contemplated setting down in Egypt before he dismissed that options as cowardice. Instead, he turned to what became his life's work: a programme of reform and education within his community. The only hope for Indian Muslims, he argued, was to acquire the intellectual merits of the people who had defeated them, a scientific temperament, modern academic culture and versatility in English language.

During the time the revolt broke out in Meerut, Sir Syed was in Bijnore, but soon thereafter he moved to Meerut. At Meerut he learnt that the soldiers of the Government had plundered his house in Delhi. The British recapture of Delhi led to ......massacre of Muslims and many innocent people were brutally put to death by the blood thirsty British. His family in Delhi paid a heavy price for opposing the British. Sir Syed lost his maternal uncle Waheeduddin Khan and his cousin Hashmat Ali was killed by the Britishers in the post mutiny massacre.

Sir Syed's mother Aziz-un-Nisa and aunt also left their ancestral *haveli* and took shelter in a small room occupied by a destitute old woman called Zebun. They remained there for eight days and passed this time under great hardship. In the meanwhile, Sir Syed also found them. He came to know that for three days, they ate nothing except the grains for horses. For two days they were without water and were very thirsty. Sir Syed went out in search of water. He could not find anything by which he could draw water from the well. He went inside the Red Fort and took from there a pitcher full of water. Reaching near his house he found the old woman, Zebun sitting on the road. She was very nervous. She had come out in search of water. After covering some distance she had given up and was unable to standup again. With trembling hands she poured that water into the pitcher. Some of it fell on the ground. Then, pointing towards the house, she uttered some words. Actually, she wanted to convey that his mother was thirsty and she wanted to take water for her and that is why she had poured water in the pitcher. He told her that he had enough water and she could drink it. He again poured water in that cup. After drinking it, she lay down on the road. He ran to the house and gave some water to his mother and aunt. They drank and thanked to God.

Sir Syed came out of the house to arrange for some carriage to take his mother and aunt to Meerut. When he came out he found Zebun dead. He could not get any carriage, though the officers had issued orders to that effect. Ultimately the officers took that coach, came to his house and went to Meerut with his mother and aunt. Due to hunger and thirst, Sir Syed's mother had developed serious bilious ailment. She was unable to digest any eatable or medicine. Thus, suffering from this disease she died in Meerut on Ist Rabi II 1274 A.H.

In this connection, *Shamsul-Ulama* Khan Bahadur Maulvi Zakaullah, who has written the biography of a Sir Syed's close friend, Maulvi Samiullah Khan, sheds some more light as follows:

> "Though making an arrangement for conveyance during that critical period was a tough job, Maulvi Samiullah hired two chariots at comparatively very high rates of fare. In one of them, sat his family-members and with another empty chariot, he went to Sir Syed's house. He requested Sir Syed's family to board the chariot. Sir Syed's wife and three children did board the chariot, though after much repeated request, but his mother and aunt refused point-blank. Anyway, Maulvi Samiullah went to Nizamuddin on foot with the chariots. This act of Samiullah left a deep impression on Sir Syed. Their friendship got also more strengthened as compared to others in the course of time".

Maulana Altaf Husain Hali has drawn a sketch of the horrifying event of 1857 in Sir Syed's biography *Hayat-e-Javed* in the following words:

> "Muslim families in Delhi, Moradabad and Bijnor had been completely devastated; Sir Syed saw it all, but was as helpless and restless as the one a part of whose house is engulfed in flames and who is running helter-skelter to fetch some water to save the rest. The government had turned completely hostile to Muslims of the country. The retaliatory actions and unimaginable atrocities inflicted in the aftermath of the revolt had left no ray of hope for the Muslims for any favour from the British Raj. Muslims were regarded as the bitterest enemies by the Britishers. British newspapers were full of anti-Muslim propaganda on a routine basis to add fuel to the fire. Courts and offices were devoid of Muslims. For them, there were few chances to join the army. In matters of visiting the royal palaces, Muslims were ignored outright. These conditions were ample proof that Muslims in India had lost the right to a peaceful and respectable life. With this situation, Sir Syed got so disheartened as to migrate to some Muslim country and be settled there. At last, however, he changed his mind and jumped into the fire in order to save the burning community".

Sir Syed says: "After the revolt, what grieved me most was not the destruction and plundering of my house, but the devastation of the community. The condition of Muslims was unbearable for me which kept me occupied for some days. Believe me, the impact was so heavy that it sapped my energy and turned my hair gray".

He was so depressed by the events of 1857 that he contemplated setting down in Egypt before he dismissed that options as cowardice. Instead, he turned to what became his life's work: a programme of reform and education within his community. The only hope for Indian Muslims, he argued, was to acquire the intellectual merits of the people who had defeated them, a scientific temperament, modern academic culture and versatility in English language.

If there had been no mutiny in 1857 and had his mother not undergone those turmoils, Sir Syed might not have been inclined towards the mission of educational upliftment of Indian community; but he would have in all likelihood preoccupied himself in writing and compiling books and in enjoying a prosperous life as a government servant. Whatever befell Sir Syed's mother shocked him severely. Sir Syed, himself, has given an account of the condition of his mother Azeezun Nisa Begum in *Seerat-e-Faridiyah*. Sir Syed's father Muhammed Muttaqui was a Mughal bureaucrat. He had served briefly as Prime Minister to Akbar II in 1815, but devoted more of his time to mystic contemplation. When he was formally admitted as a disciple of Shah Ghulam Ali, his father lost interest in household matters. Therefore, much of the credit for Sir Syed's training and moral education goes to his mother. She possessed exceptional abilities as compared to other women. She knew how to read the Holy Quran and had also studied some Persian books in her early years. Sir Syed can never forget the experience he had in his mother's lap. His very first teacher was none other than his mother. She also used to teach the girls of the relatives and the neighbourhood.

Recalling his mother's exhortations, Sir Syed says: "When I was posted in Delhi as a *Munsif*, my mother always advised me to use conveyance as well as to walk sometimes to my destination. She said that one should not rely on changing conditions and circumstances; I should develop the habit which I could continue with. Therefore, whenever I went to the *Jama Masjid* or the *Khanqah*, it was by means of any conveyance or on foot".

"My mother always kept 5 percent of the income for charitable purposes. Many young girls were married due to her financial help. She secretly helped financially distressed veiled women. She advised poor young widows for remarriage. She despised those who did not like a second marriage for widows. She visited poor relatives and secretly helped them. Some of the relatives had married women who were not considered respectable. She often visited their houses and treated their children with kindness.

Apart from determination, large- heartedness and human kindness, Sir Syed also found broad-mindedness with regard to religious concerns from her mother. She did not like traditional customs and had little faith in amulets and spiritual practices".

Sir Syed's sister, Safiyyatun-Nisa Begum was a distinguished lady. Fond of religious books, she often studied some Arabic books of Hadith (Traditions of Prophet Muhammad—pbuh) with translation. Generally, girls of the families of the relatives would gather to take lessons from her.

Khwaja Altaf Hussain Hali has mentioned the name of Sir Syed's elder sister as Safiyyatun-Nisa, whereas Sir Syed, himself has mentioned her in his own writings as Ujbatun-Nisa Begum. Sir Syed wrote about her in respect to women's education: "The residence of my sister was dedicated for this purpose, and a group of girls would get education in the verandah. My brother-in-law, who was a scholar of religious education, would cooperate in every way possible in the same direction. The real brother of my maternal grandfather would visit the school daily or on alternate days and taught Persian style of writing to girls. From morning to afternoon, it was study time. All the girls would take lunch with the landlady of the house. Therefore, they learnt how to weave and sew and various other household tasks up to the time of *Zuhr* (noon) Prayer. After Prayer, there again started classes up to the time of *Asr* (evening) Prayer.

Having offered *Asr* Prayer, all the girls would return to their houses. Friday used to be a gala day. All the girls would come as usual in the morning and together they prepared different dishes in small cooking vessels and enjoyed them. Sometimes, their brothers of their age would accompany them too".

That was the kind of education Sir Syed deemed essential for women of the east. Seeing the plight and prejudice against Indian women, he was often annoyed and grudged it. In the 19th century Indian society, female infanticide and *Sati* system were under prevalence. Worse enough, marriage of a girl to more than one man was in practice. Sir Syed launched a campaign for purging the society of all the prevailing evils, especially for abolishing illiteracy and ignorance. At the very outset, he struck at the roots of superstition. He delivered a lecture on July 5, 1866, at the Institute of Scientific Society. Based on the idea of the well-being of the fellow-countrymen, the lecture appeared in the *Aligarh Institute Gazette*, on July 13, 1866. Originally, the lecture was in Urdu, whereas its English version was prepared by Syed Mahmud. Focusing on diverse issues such as polygamy, the tradition of *Sati*, murdering of girls and ill treatment of women, etc., Sir Syed says, "Of all the evil traditions, the most notorious ones were performing *Sati* and taking a dying person to the bank of a pond and murder him forcibly. As for foeticide (mostly in the form of abortion) and spending money extravagantly on the occasion of marriage, unfortunate all that can be seen till date. Of these practices, killing of girl babies or foetuses is so heinously powerful that it dwarfs not only the human instinct of adopting good moral values but also puts a check to the development of a creature. As a result, a community or a nation can never attain its glory or an increment thereof. In this regard, no advice or exhortation would prove to be fruitful. A law, banning polytheism, is the only remedy for which a petition has already been filed".

The Indians had started taking interest in education largely due to the promotion of western ideology and the occupation of the country by the English. Many educational centres came into being in different areas. The issue of women's education got considerable attention and was brought under consideration. People began expressing their views in favour of women's education. For Sir Syed, these developments were indicative of some great change. He said in the address mentioned above: “Many of the Madrasas or collages have been opened up in different places by Muslims such as in metroes like Calcutta (Kolkata), Lahore, Agra and Ghazipur. Also, women’s education (is going on), be it at home or Madrasas. All this is without an iota of doubt and needs no proof”.

Sir Syed expressed his views extensively on women’s education through many articles and editorials. A good number of issues of the *Institute Gazette* and *Tahzeebul-Akhlaq* are sufficient proof. Sir Syed proved before the Hunter Education Commission that the notion that Muslim women were not educated was wrong. For this, he had cited the examples of women of his own family. His beloved granddaughter, i.e., Syed Hamid’s only daughter, Ahmadeen Begum, used to have postal communication with her grandfather, Sir Syed Ahmad Khan, at an early age of about twelve. These letters also testify that girls of his family were all educated.

Sir Syed-the pioneer of Aligarh movement while in favour of Western education for men was only modesty reformist when it came to women. Although he argued that *Purdah* (veil) was not sanctioned by Islam nor was the denial of female education, it was his view that women’s education was to emphasize moral and spiritual values. No doubt, Sir Syed seems to be all praise and appreciation for women. He never ignored issues concerning women’s education and their proper training. He appreciated and acknowledged heartily those whom he found to be active regarding women’s education.

He regarded the spread of education the only means for progress. He told the Indians not to strive for anything other then education which was the root of progress. Hence since the beginning he started pleading for education and repeatedly told India ‘cure the roots, and the tree will itself flourish’. As education has always been an instrument of producing a more enlightened atmosphere, it may help men in distinguishing between good or evil. It may reform his morals and solve his problems.

Sir Syed had thoroughly studied India's socio-economic and political problems and as a reformer, he suggested its remedy also which was nothing but education. He urged the Indians to establish schools without Government support and interference and according to the own liking. He said that "to understand the principles of our British Government defective is because of the lack of higher education. As the higher education will advance we will understand those principles and respect them. If the Government has not given our rights to us, education is such a thing which may provide us our rights".

He wanted Indians to start on their own feet, create self-confidence and not beg the Government for small things. He wished that the Muslim community should start big colleges and universities for the education of the downtrodden members.

Commenting on Sir Syed's policy of women's education, Prof. Shameem Nikhat opines: "Sir Syed's chief motto was to educate Muslims morally, socially and intellectually. He knew well the fact that his dream could not be materialised unless women, along with men, were empowered with education and their religious faiths and practices, corrected. That is why Sir Syed started writing in *Tahzeebul Akhlaq,* in 1870, on varied subjects such as women's education, polygamy and general well-being. Soon, a circle of bright and broad-minded Muslims was formed. They all laid emphasis on education for Muslims, particularly women's education and personality development. In 1904, the first ever women's conference was held at Aligarh by the good offices of Shaikh Abdullah and, a decision was taken with regard to women's emancipation".

As part of Sir Syed's movement, when the efforts were made to impart knowledge of English language to Muslim boys, a *fatwa* (a religious decree) was issued by some *Ulama* condemning the instruction of English. The *Fatwa* read: "Learning English language is tantamount to committing apostasy (*kufr*). In that critical period, what to mention of girls' education, even that of boys was a great challenge. As for Hindu society, many girls' schools had been opened under the influence of the awareness campaigns, launched by Brahmo Samaj, Arya Samaj, Prarthna Samaj and leaders like Maharshi Kurde, etc. But what proved to be the greatest obstacle for Muslim girls was the abandoning of veil. In the north Indian Hindu society, too, the practice of covering the face in public places was in vogue ....In this context, getting education in a school was equal to converting to Christianity.

Sir Syed had blown the trumpet to equip Indian Muslims with modern education soon after the great revolution of 1857. For his mission to succeed, he needed to see the functioning of modern universities in UK. It was first his luck that the British Government sanctioned nine scholarships of six thousand rupees each for bright students to get higher education in Britain. Apart from that, the British Government also sanctioned three thousand rupees for travelling expenses. The U.P. Government nominated Sir Syed's son, Syed Mahmood for this scholarship. Accompanying his son, he went abroad to see these universities in the West. This expedition consisted of five persons, namely, Sir Syed, both his sons — Syed Hamid and Syed Mahmood, Mirza Khuda Dad Beg and a personal attendant Chhajju. Sir Syed mortgaged his Aligarh's house to Maulvi Samiullah Khan to meet the expanses and even disposed of his precious collection of books at low prices.

On his way to Britain, Sir Syed happened to see Miss Marie Carpenter. Miss Carpenter was well known for her philanthropy and her efforts in the cause of female education in Calcutta and Bombay. Sir Syed had long and interesting conversations with her upon female education, as well as upon other important issues. Miss Carpenter was a native of Bristol, daughter of Dr. Carpenter, and she has made herself famous in her native town by her efforts in educating the children of the poor. Raja Ram Mohan Roy, the Unitarian, was a great friend of hers, and he died at her father's house whilst on a visit.

It was his description of the sad state of Indian women that prompted her voyage to India. She had a note book with her containing opinions on the state of Indian women by many influential personalities, and she asked Sir Syed to contribute as well. He wrote: "En route to London I have made the acquaintance of Miss Carpenter- an acquaintance which honours and gives me the highest pleasure. Since I first heard her name in connection with her efforts for the advancement of Indian women, I have been desirous of making her acquaintance. Thanks to God, that pleasure has now been vouchsafed to me. "Her lofty aims, keen insight, and goodness of heart are evidenced by her efforts in the cause of Indian women." To work for the education of women, whom God had made as a helpmate to men in good works, is worthy of every praise. To do good in every way is most laudable, as, if the foundation is good, good results must follow. Even if mistakes be made at the commencement, efforts thus made excite the emulation of others, and the right results will ensure. Efforts for good are sometimes frustrated owing to their being contrary to the manners and customs of those for who's good they are intended.

In such cases, it is like going contrary to nature; and by doing so; one may prevent any good results. I trust and hope that Miss Carpenter's endeavours may be crowned with success, and the men and women of India, will have their hearts enlightened by truth and culture.

Nevertheless, I wish Miss Carpenter all success and fruition in her mission. I wish both Indian men and women get enlightened from the light of Truth and Knowledge, without prejudice".

These lines hold the pointer to the fact that Sir Syed looked upon men and women as fellow-strugglers of life and valued the efforts in educating women. At the same time, he also acknowledged the bottlenecks that hinder the progress and for the removal of which though more time was required, continued struggle was of great importance. According to Sir Syed, "Persistence with efforts is the key to success!"

During his journey to London, he also happened to see a Muslim foster mother, named Naseeban, a maid servant of Mrs.

Couper, the wife of the Deputy Commissioner of Lucknow, was on board, and she was a wonderful person in her own way. She belonged to an Afghan Pathan family and a resident of Kanpur. She told Sir Syed this was her twenty- first trip to Europe, being always employed in attending on children. She knew English well, and had been to England, Scotland, Ireland, France, Portugal and other countries. He thought to himself that she was better than most of the men. Sir Syed expressed his happiness in the following words: She is no less wonderful than the Suez Canal and said to her "Well done, you are indeed greater than men".

Sir Syed visited the museum of Versailles Palace on May 2, 1869. But he was deeply hurt when he saw one of the paintings of the wars in Algeria. In the painting he saw the ladies of the family of Syed Abdul Qadir al-Jazairi depicted in a very pitiable condition. They were prisoners. The French solders had made their camels sit down and brought down their litters. The ladies had fallen off down their litters. The ladies had fallen off from them with their bodies getting uncovered. The French soldiers stood with their bayonets pointing towards them. Mentioning this painting, Sir Syed writes that the pitiable condition of the helpless women depicted in it would be enough to make any self respecting Muslim weep. He says that it is shameful for Frenchmen to depict those women in such a disgraceful semi nude condition and also to think that the painting is meant to be a tribute to the valour of the French army. It puts a stain on the refinement of the culture of the French people. Then he says, "This picture does not evoke any contempt for Imam Abdul Qadir, On the contrary it elicits the same kind of respect in the hearts which existed during the days of his rule over Algeria. For 20-30 years he alone thought with great valour against the mighty French Empire. He always remained true to his words, never deceived his enemy and after his defeat he fulfilled all the conditions of the peace treaty till the last moment of his life".

In Paris, Sir Syed was deeply touched by the etiquette of a sales girl in a shop. She was clad in decent and attractive clothes and was speaking English in a very sweet and civilized manner. She helped Sir Syed and his companions wear the gloves. In Paris, it was a custom to wear gloves before going to dinner, meeting ladies and visiting Heads of State. Sir Syed writes: "That lady knew four languages — French, English, Italian and German and was well-versed in all the four. She had learnt the languages so that she may talk easily with the customers of those countries".

During his stay in London, Sir Syed was highly impressed with the etiquette and skills of some European women. The house, part of which Sir Syed had hired during his stay, belonged to Mr. J. Ludlam. Six rooms of that house were occupied by Sir Syed—four bed rooms for four different persons, one drawing room and another dining room. Mr. Ludlam was a highly qualified person and was an expert in many fields. In leisure hours at night, he delivered lectures on Chemistry, Geology, Zoology, etc. His wife was accomplished on domestic matters. She was such a qualified and cultured lady that according to Sir Syed, "words cannot describe her qualities. She was the embodiment of manners, etiquette, ethics and humanity. She performed all the household chores herself very efficiently."

The two sisters of Mrs. Ludlam, Miss Ellen West and Miss Fanny West were also like her. One of them Ellen West was a bookworm. She often took Sir Syed's books even during illness. For Sir Syed, it was an unforgettable experience to see a woman studying books even during illness and being ready to review them: "This gives rise to the reflection of how good the education of women of the middle class must be here. It is not a matter for astonishment that a woman, when ill, should read with the object of improving her mind?

Under the impact of these women's education and decency, Sir Syed compares and contrasts European women with their Indian counterparts in his travelogue: "Now, it must be realised that women belonging to lower middle class are highly educated. Is it not a matter of surprise that a woman garners interest in reading a book during illness? Have you ever seen a rich man, a *nawab*, a king or any noble person doing that?

If a woman walks through a market-place all naked, how ashamed and surprised our compatriots would feel. No exaggeration, it is a fact that when women in Europe hear of Indian women who do not know even the three R's and have no sense how to represent themselves, they are surprised in the same way, and they are filled with hatred."

Sir Syed had also two maidservants at his disposal for domestic chores that were provided by the kind- hearted landlady. They were Anne Smith and Elizabeth Matthews. These maids were punctual and honest to their jobs and rendered their services well. They impressed Sir Syed by their education, honesty and decency. He mentions his views at length in a letter to his friend Raja Jai Kishan Das with much enthusiasm: "If one meets women of big families in India, one would find them to be just animals and have one's heart filled with hatred towards them. All this is because of (lack of) education."

He writes about the young girl, Elizabeth Matthews, "who in spite of her poverty, invariably buys a halfpenny paper called the "Echo", and reads it when at leisure. If she comes across a "Punch" in which there are pictures of women's manners and customs, she looks at them, and enjoys the editor's remarks thereon. Until the education of the masses is pushed on as it is here, it is impossible for a native to become civilized and honoured".

During his stay in London for seventeen months, Sir Syed seems to be all praise for the European ladies. At the same time, he seems to be greatly pleased with Muslim women's education and etiquette in Egypt and Turkey. He mentions about a Muslim Turkish girl: "Education is increasing day after day in both Egypt and Rome. Women are also getting education. I have heard of a Muslim girl from Egypt who can speak French fluently and understands besides Arabic, Latin well to explain any verse or article. Her brother was educated in France. When he returned home, she learnt French and Latin from him. It was this girl who had already learnt, from elder members of the family, how to read and write Arabic effectively because she was very enthusiastic about education."

Sir Syed also visited Cambridge and Oxford universities and studied their management and system. Then he made an assessment of education in general, observed the system of women's education and noted in particular the method of education which he thought to be suitable for Indian Muslims. In the words of Mohsinul Mulk: "This man was sent abroad (by Allah) for the benevolence of the community, as was his stay and return. While staying in London itself, he had drawn up a plan to establish a Muslim University in India. He knew that making organisations would be of no use for the betterment of social and political condition of Muslims. He regarded this act as an attempt to cross a river with a boat made of paper. All the efforts to improve the condition of Muslims could only be successful only by imparting them the knowledge of English education. Without English, all attempts would prove to be futile like watering a field before sowing seed.

Sir Syed Ahmed had also prepared a 29-point charter in order to create a better social code and remove all the social evils from amongst Muslims. Of them, three points were especially concerned with women's education. He wanted that girls should be educated as well as be trained in various skills. He emphasised that women should be treated well and respectfully. He was also against polygamy in spite of Islamic permission for four marriages, as Sir Syed opined that abstaining from polygamy is better than disobeying Allah's commandments regarding equal treatment of more than one wives".

Tahzeeb-ul- Akhlaq by Sir Syed Ahmed Khan played the same role in spreading awareness among the masses as had been done by the *Spectator and Tatler* in the 18th century London. These two magazines miraculously helped in abolishing the age-old traditions of London and created a keen sense of decency and moral values.

During his stay in London, Sir Syed had also the privilege to see Queen Victoria twice. First, on November 1869 on the occasion of inauguration ceremony of a bridge and then on March 11, 1870 in Her Excellency's palace, where Sir Syed kissed the Queen's hand as well. The Queen was younger to Sir Syed by two years. He says that the credit for Queen's grandeur and dignity goes to the education provided by her kind mother. In memory of the Queen, Sir Syed held inauguration ceremony of his school on May 24, 1875, the date of her birth.

If we study the letters written by Sir Syed, it becomes clear that by 1869, articles had started to be published in periodicals regarding women's education. On October 22, 1869, Sir Syed wrote a letter from London: "To the best of my knowledge, no such a truthful and excellent article regarding women's education has so far appeared in any magazine or newspaper." He says further: "Therefore, what is the obstacle for Indian Muslims and Hindus to make provision to educate their girls with freedom, and instill in them respective moral values? Is India unable to do that? No, it is not. India is, in no way, unable to impart women's education, rather missions of greater magnitude than that can be achieved. What are required are determination, boldness and interest.

So, hopefully you would not bank upon others for the good of Indian masses. All that apart, you must encourage your brothers to take such initiatives on their own. You ought to remember, "Allah helps those who help themselves."

The letters of Sir Syed, too, indicate his eagerness and restlessness as regards women's education. He urged that both Hindus and Muslim should start schools for girls' education.

While in London, Sir Syed reflected on the political degradation, educational and civilizational backwardness, prevailing sense of hopelessness, economic, crisis and political anarchy in India. He thought only Western education could better the situation. He made people realise the necessity to change their thinking and lifestyle in keeping with the need of the hour.

On the 24th May 1875, a school, named Madarsatul Uloom Muslamanan-e-Hind came into being with, thanks to the good offices of Sir Syed Ahmad Khan and his friends at Aligarh but actual work commenced on the Ist. June, 1875 when some of the school classes were started. On the 12th November of the same year Sir William Muir visited the Primary Madarsa and a grand reception was given to him. The founder requested Lady Muir to plant a sapling in the park inaugurated after her name. In other words, status of women was recognized in the very early period of the Madarsa.

Emphasising women's education among Muslims, Sir William Muir said that: "I have often while in these provinces lamented the custom by which the females of India are left in ignorance, and have urged upon you the necessity, if you would really seek to elevate the social position of the people, of educating your girls. And here once more I would advert to the subject, for I feel persuaded that until this is done, no real advance will be permanently secured. I lately saw in the papers the account of an excellent school established at Cairo by one of the wives of his Highness the Khedive of Egypt. This lady hired a lady from Syria, called Sitt Rosa, with a staff of teachers. There are 200 boarders and 100 day-scholars; and they are taught all kinds of needle work, European and Oriental, besides reading and writing and useful knowledge. As I read, I thought to myself-would that some native lady in these provinces might follow this example! Such, now, is a specimen of the way in which each and all of you might become useful to your fellow-countrymen.

I hope that all these things encourage you in this direction and education spreads far and wide. O youths! Take care of good conduct and character. Remember, man becomes a man not just by education but by other attributes such as honesty, good character, God worshipping, etc. Both these two qualities must be identified by this college and by virtue of them; the college should be recognised across the world."

On the occasion of the foundation stone-laying ceremony of Muhammadan Anglo-Oriental College, on January 8, 1877, Lord Lytton, Viceroy and Governor-General of India was invited. At Sir Syed's House, Mrs. Downe, who was part of the delegation headed by the Viceroy, also accompanied Mrs. Viceroy during the refreshment and they held discussions with Sir Syed.

The Chief Guest on that gala occasion was Lord Lytton, but the first stone was laid by Mrs. Lytton. For that, Khan Bahadur Muhammed Hayat Khan also thanked her.

Sir John Strachey visited Aligarh along with his wife on December 10, 1880. His wife was a known artist. She also sketched a portrait of Sir Syed with oil colours. For this, Sir Syed had often to go to Allahabad and pose before the artist. It indicates that Sir Syed was fairly a broad-minded and modern man.

The Principal of M.A.O. College and a majority of teachers were the products of either Cambridge or Oxford University. Their wives also resided with them in the thatched bungalows on the college campus engaged in bringing up young generations being loyal to the British. However many revolutionaries and radicals emerged from the same generations. On certain important occasions, Sir Syed sought advice from them. These ladies had played a significant role on the campus life. Teachers and students of the colleges were welcomed and hosted by these ladies, and were impressed by their lifestyle. The wives of these British teachers of Aligarh used that to college students in the same patronizing manner as the wives of British Civil Servants. These English women enjoyed horse riding as well as taught English to some students, too. Mrs. Theodore Morison had also started taking class to teach letter writing in English at her bungalow. The students included Sajjad Haider Yaldrem, Abu Muhammed Ijaz Ali, Muhammed Zareef and Sir Raza Ali. Off and on, Meer Vilayat Husain and Syed Jalaluddin Haider also attended these informal classes. On the recommendation of Theodore Morison, when Syed Raza Ali was appointed a government servant at Saharanpur, he was invited to lunch by Mr. Morison and his wife.

Our forefathers had studied in Aligarh when the British power and glory was at its zenith. Although they had received their education at the feet of these imperialist British teachers, they used to celebrate the victory of Japan and Turkey over the British.

On the occasion of completion of seven years of the Siddons Club, a celebration was held in which all the European ladies were also invited. Sir Syed too attended the party. During that period, the College's Principal Mr. Theodore Beck returned to Aligarh from London with his wife for the first time. On this occasion, a student, viz, Khushi Muhammad recited a poem welcoming Mrs. Beck: 'Tonight our guest is Mrs. Beck to whom the union extends a warm welcome'.

In November 1892, Siddons Club organised a function in the honour of Professor T.W. Arnold. After his marriage in London on February 29, 1892, he had brought his wife also to Aligarh (On this occasion, a verse was read out in their honour): "Mr. Arnold has come to India from London and has brought an angel in the human form."

The wife of M.A.O. College Principal Theoder Beck took great interest in the College affairs. She played a significant role in appointing Mrs. Griffiths the Lady Superintendent of the new Hostel for English House Boarding. Unfortunately, Indian climate did not suit her and in 1904, Miss. Harris was then appointed the lady Superintendent of the Boys' Hostel in her place. The resignation of Miss Harris, Lady Superintendent was accepted by the syndicate on February 21, 1915, and she left Aligarh on April 25. Miss Hannah Beck, sister of the late Principal Beck, arrived in October, 1915 to succeed Miss Harris.

Ladies of European Professors had established such firm relations with some of the students that they not only taught them English on their bungalows but also entertained them with tea and cakes. Record indicates that Mrs Morison continued to take letter-writing classes at her residence every Wednesday evening and get their work corrected.

In the third Session of Muslim Educational Conference, held in 1888 in Lahore, Sir Syed says: "With the cooperation of my friends, I have seen, in London, girls' schools wherein girls belonging to noble families reside and study. Believe me, the standard of quality, satisfaction and education I've observed in those schools, India would take hundreds of years to reach."

Elaborating on his views, he writes to the Editor of *Tahzeeb-e-Niswan*, published from Lahore, Syed Mumtaz Ali, "It is my cordial desire that women should also be given standard and higher education, but in the present scenario, educating unmarried girls is equal to torturing and assaulting them. Their education before converting men into civilized human beings is by no means appropriate; rather it would add fuel to the fire. For this very reason, I've done nothing so far for their education."

In the context of Sir Syed's policy of women's education, Rashid Ahmad Siddiqui, a well-known literary figure in Urdu and a brilliant student of M.A.O. College, says: "In that period, the 'swords' which he made use of as *Masaf-e-Zindagi* were largely based on Muslim boys. Probably he might have thought of Muslim girls in the way that was traditional that Muslim girls would automatically change themselves, only if boys are appropriately educated as per the need of the hour. This thought was not based on some whim because the talks, which Sir Syed held on one occasion with respect to the boys' education, were in favour of that very domestic system of education that was in vogue in the noble families of his period in Delhi. Maybe, he was sure that his opponents might turn even more hostile to his cause on talking of girls' education as they had already disapproved strongly the idea of new educational system even for boys. That is why he focused his attention on boys only. Probably, Sir Syed was aware of the strategy that during war, every precaution must be taken to make assaults on the weakest possible fronts. It was this critical moment when Shaikh Abdullah, a disciple of Sir Syed stood for the cause of girls' education and brought some ray of hope".

Sir Syed Ahmad Khan was a staunch supporter of girls' education but he did not pay his attention towards it because of certain bottlenecks in his mission. On this basis, some regarded him as an opponent of girls' education.

None but Shaikh Abdullah himself writes blaming Sir Syed: "Even a great national leader like Sir Syed opposed the cause of modern education for girls who went on opposing throughout his life....On the one hand, there were some efforts for boys' English education, on the other hand, even making a mention of girls' education in his presence was difficult. Whenever I heard Sir Syed talking on education, he always condemned girls' English education. Just as the Muslim *Ulema* considered education of English for boys to be an act of apostasy, similarly, Sir Syed regarded English education for girls to be harmful for their moral character".

In his autobiography, *Mushahidat-o-Taassurat* (observations and views) Shaikh Muhammed Abdullah makes mentions of some events when he was a student in 1896: "In that period, word went round regarding girls' education. Nawab Mohsin-ul-Mulk approved of the idea. I personally know that Sir Syed was against starting any school for girls or any other new system of education for them. He never wished girls to be independent like boys after getting education at schools. He had no justification whatsoever for his stand. In the light of my personal knowledge about Sir Syed's life, I find no wisdom in his viewpoint. I thought and still think that Sir Syed was under the influence of traditions in this respect, in particular. He supported the most radical and conservative mind as regards observing veil. He was much apprehensive that after getting education, girls would abandon veil. He respected veil very much.

This is a misconceived notion that Sir Syed was opposed to female education. Actually it was not so. The question of education of males was to him a matter of preference. He appreciated the efforts of Miss Carpenter, who was anxious to promote education among Indian women. In his *Aligarh Institute Gazette* he repeatedly wrote on the problems of women's education and invited the attention of his countrymen to the same. He rebutted the remark that women were inferior to men and pleaded equal treatment for them. In 1870 Sir Syed started *Tehzeeb-ul-Akhlaq* and wrote much on women's education. He also expressed that had there been girls school in India like those in England, he would have advised every family to send their daughters to such schools.

In an article on the rights of women, Sir Syed says: "The religion of Islam confers respect on women and recognizes the right and powers to be equal to men to an extent that it is not to be found in this measure even today in any civilized country. Islamic law recognizes equality of men and women in their rights and power".

In his article, he has shed light on women's right: "Here we are to discuss the good treatment of women by men. They should pay attention to treat them well. They should be courteous, hospitable, considerate and loving, and provide them with enjoyment, comfort, happiness and pleasure; and keep them happy in all respect. And instead of considering them as servants they should take them as friends and companions and as those who share both in distress and comfort and consider that both men and women provide happiness and encouragement to each other".

On analysing Sir Syed's articles and speeches, the fact comes to the fore that he was not against women's education. But he was helpless in the face of stark opposition by the *Ulema*. So, he always tried not to add fuel to the fire by talking of women's education. Sir Syed had also studied the history of all the civilized nations of the world and he was sure that girls' education will automatically start once boys' education picks up. Therefore, he focused mainly on boys' education. In 1882, the statement which Sir Syed gave before the Education Commission under the chairmanship of W.W. Hunter, it is evident that he had pleaded the cause of women's education strongly and discussed every dimension thereof freely like an expert on education.

By the efforts of Sir Syed a vigorous campaign for the dissemination of modern education among the males was set into motion at the Muslim Educational Conference. Women's education was still obscure and it was only in 1888 that Zanana madarsas were discussed. In 1891, Khwaja Ghulam-us Saqlain (1871-1915), a student of the MAO College, Aligarh made such an impressive speech in support of a resolution of women's education that Sir Syed embraced him and announced that he was not opposed to women's education and a section for women's education was created within the Mohammadan Educational Conference.

Reacted on the resolution moved by Khawaja Ghulam-us–Saqlain, Sir Syed pointed out: "whatever education is being given to male is actually meant for the ladies also. Men's education is actually a means of female education. Unless males are competent, females can not be so...we do not claim. Prophethood neither can we prophecy. But we must learn things from the history of the past. When we study the history of the whole Europe and the countries which are educationally advanced, we find that when men are educated, women are also educated. This is the reason why we do not consider the question of women's education exclusively. But whatever we are doing for male education is meant for the women folk also. Let me cite you some examples of the European communities where men are ignorant and women are also the same, both suffer for many aberrations and superstitions so much that on the doors of their houses, the horseshoes are screwed to get rid of ignorance. But in those communities where men are educated, women have also been provided education... If you know the conditions of India tell me why the ladies of those families were so highly educated. There is a saying that the blessings of God do not ascend from the earth but descend from the sky. The sunlight too never comes from the earth but from the sky. Similarly female education comes from male education. To blame me for ignoring female education is wrong. Men do not understand that their education is actually a means for women education. If men are uneducated neither will there be lady teachers nor other paraphernalia. When men will become competent, they will provide all means of education to females. Housewives will become good and lady teachers will also come out of it. When they (husbands) will be educated, they will arrange for the education of their wives. You search those means of education for your women which are opposed to history. I follow those ways which are in harmony with the law of Nature".

Sir Syed had studied the British history of female education which was not common towards the end of the eighteenth and early nineteenth centuries. Deborah Simonthon in her article on 'women and education in England' highlights the stages through which women's education had passed. She says that girls were thought at home and were "expected to focus their life on the world of house and home, while their brothers anticipated a life of work, politics and public affairs. This contrast between male and female was probably more pronounced in the middle and upper classes... Maternal affection and the perceived need to shelter and protect young women may have contributed to the tendency to keep girls at home".

In the Panjab, he was invited by the wife of Sardar Muhammad Hayat Khan in 1884 at Gurudaspur to address a gathering under the banner of *Khawateen-e-Panjab* (Punjab's Women). They wanted to know directly his view about women's education. This was the first speech in the history of India in which the Hindu, Muslim, Sikhs and Christian ladies were addressed by the great social reformer, Sir Syed Ahmad Khan.

He addressed thus: "My sisters! To meet you this night is no less than a *Shab-i-Qadr* (a blessed night). The Address presented to me by you is a matter of great honour which, so far none has received in India. I am heartily thankful to you for this kindness.

O my sisters! I have great respect for the women of my community. The male members of my community have completely ruined the fair name of their ancestors. But by the grace of God, you still possess the qualities of our ancestors. This is a fact that among the male members we do not have a Shibli or a Junaid, but thanks to God that there are thousands of Rabia Basris among you.

O my sisters! I am not mindless of the education of the women of my community. I heartily want them to receive education. But I am opposed to that system of education towards which short sighted people are inclined. I advise you to try to adopt your old system of education. Only that method will benefit you in this world as well as in the hereafter and will protect you from hazards".

After that Sir Syed gave a detailed description of the old system of education for women. He said, "My sisters! Believe me there is not a single nation in the world in which the condition of women might have improved before the improvement in the condition of men. Similarly, there is not a single nation in which the condition of men had improved; while that of the women remained stagnant. These phenomena have greatly influenced me. From my efforts for boys' education, you should not conclude that I have forgotten my dear daughters. I believe that making endeavours for the education of boys amounts to laying the base for female education. Thus; the service which I am doing for boys is actually service to both the boys as well as the girls.

I do not want you to read the fast spreading abominable books of the present times in place of the sacred books which were read by your grandmothers. The men who earn bread for you, due to the force of circumstances may have to acquire new learning or learn a new language or adopt a new mode, but the change of circumstances has not necessitated any changes in your educational requirements.

It is imperative for you to know your religion; you should know its virtues as well as the merits of worshipping God; you should understand the value of gentle manners of kindness, love and compassion; you should put these qualities into practice in your daily life; keep the domestic management in your hands, be the mistress of your house, govern your house like a princess and manage it like a capable minister, bring up your children, make your daughters like yourself by educating them, worship God and fear Him, be sympathetic towards your neighbours. All these beneficial aspects of education are learnt very well from the books that your grandmothers used to read. They are beneficial even now as they were during those times of your grandmothers. Thus why should you read the objectionable books being written now? It is true that due to the depravity and ignorance of the male members of your family, many such rights which God has bestowed on you and which, on humanitarian grounds, you deserve to possess, have not been given to you. The device by which you may get back those rights is to try to educate the boys of your family. When they shall become educated, you would get back your rights, usurped by men without your asking for them.

At the end, Sir Syed addressing the Hindu and Christian ladies said, "My Hindu and Christian sisters! You joined along with your Muslim sisters in the Address presented to me and also contributed to the aid given to the poor students of the Madarsat-ul-Uloom out of your compassion and feeling of national unity. This gesture shows your compassion and feeling of amity. I heartily thank you for this and pray to God that He may shower His blessings on you and you may be blessed with all round progress and happiness. *Ameen*".

The above speech indicates that the visionary Sir Syed was not against women's education. In fact, he wanted to take up this issue only after the successful launch of boys' education. He expressed the hope that only by the spread of education among men; women would get back, without their asking for them, their rights which were usurped by the former.

In an article, published in *Tahzeebul Akhlaq*, Sir Syed wrote with reference to women's education, "Those who blame Islam for all these evil practices are certainly in the wrong. The fact is that main cause of women's degradation, in India, is the inability of Muslims to obey the religious injunctions. If all the injunctions of Islam are duly obeyed, all the social evils will be removed without an iota of doubt. Apart from that, another chief reason is the uncivilized way of life. Civilized people have placed their women on a high pedestal in spite of their weak and faulted social system. On the contrary, Muslims whose rules and regulations are the best of all have made the condition of their women very deplorable and pathetic because of their ignorance and illiteracy. For this reason, the world laughs at them. Since all the Muslims, except a few are of the same mindset, Islam is considered to be full of faults. It is high time, therefore, that we pay serious attention on all these issues and mend our ways. Islam is the best religion; a light of guidance but we would have to prove it by our own conduct".

Emphasising on women's education, Sir Syed says in another article, "Knowledge is, no doubt, the life force for man whereas ignorance is like a death. So, what a great irony it is that people who themselves are full of enthusiasm and charm of life are a dull and passive existence. We don't mean that women should be given absolute freedom with regards to veil, etc., or are made self-dependent on getting educated and they begin reigning over men. On the contrary, what we want is just to adore them with the jewels of education without ignoring their essential traits. It will certainly lead to their betterment... Therefore, we hope our fellow citizens to make efforts for the overall development and growth of Indians with their self-encouragement and interest to partake in this programme like those gentle fellows who established *Madaris* (schools) on certain occasions".

In fact, his plan of modern education for Muslim youths had already put him in much trouble, and he was not willing to invite further wrath of the diehards of his community by speaking out for female education.

When Sir Syed launched his campaign, Islam was under threat in India from three corners. On the one hand, missionaries were ready to attack its edifice. The biggest threat was from the

Christianity. They were busy, round the clock, to defame Islam. On the second front was the political scenario. The English had taken away governance from the Muslim rulers. Therefore, Muslims were always looked down upon by them. The English termed Islam the main cause of violence and rebellion and enemy of peace. The third threat was the education of English because the missionary volunteers had forcefully entered houses and encouraged people to get English education with a view to Christianising Indian Hindus and Muslims. Sir Syed wanted to keep women away from the missionary schools until Muslim boys were fully educated along modern lines. It was the need of the hour. Noted Urdu poet; Dr. Sir Mohammed Iqbal rightly observed that Sir Syed was the first Muslim of modern times who saw a glimpse of the future. Shaikh Abdullah actually fulfilled that very dream of Sir Syed. Therefore, promotion of women's education in India is but an indispensable part of the Aligarh Movement.

References

1. Altaf Hussain Hali: Hayat-e-Javaid, p-83, Taraqqui Urdu Bureau, New Delhi-1982.
2. Hayat-i-Javed by Hali translated by Prof. Rafi Ahmad Alvi, p 37 published by Sir Syed Academy, AMU, Aligarh, 2008.
3. Maulvi Zakaullah: Sawanih Umri Haji Muahmmad Samiullah Khan, p-31. U.P. Urdu Academy, Lucknow, 1997.
4. Altaf Husain Hali: Hayat-e-Javaid, p-152.
5. Lecture—Muslim Educational Conference: 1889.
6. Syed Ahmad Khan: *Seerat-e-Faridiyah*, Mufeed Aam, Agra-1896.
7. Altaf Husain Hali: Hayat-e-Javaid, p-48.
8. Prof. Iftikhar Alam, *Sir Syed Duroon-e-Khana*, published by Educational Book House, Aligarh.

9. *Mukammal Majmua-e-Lecture Wa Speeches*, p229, by Maulvi Imamuddin Gujrati, Naval Kishore Printing Works, Lahore.
10. Aligarh Institute Gazette, July 13, 1866.
11. ibid.
12. Muhammad Samueel Falahi: Sir Syed aur Taaleem-e-Niswan, p-19, Tahzeeb Karachi, March 2005, Vol-22, No:3.
13. Prof. Iftikhar Aalam: Sir Syed Duroon-e-Khana, p-28, Mahnama Nawa-e-Akhlaq, Ravalpindi, April-2006, Vol-4, No:6.
14. Mumtaz Moin: The Aligarh Movement, p115, published by Salman Academy, Karachi.
15. Altaf Husain Hali, *Hayat-e-Javed*, p 85.
16. *Mukammal Majmua-e-Lecture Wa Speeches*, p 41, by Maulvi Imamuddin Gujrati, Naval Kishore Printing Works, Lahore.
17. Tahzibul Akhlaq, 10 Shawwal 1289 AH.
18. Munshi Sirajuddin, *Sir Syed Ke Lecturon Ka Majmua*, p 174 (1890).
19. Prof. Shameem Nikhat: Aazadi-e-Niswan ki Jadd-o-Jahad p-43, Urdu mein Nisai Adab ka Manzar Namah, Deptt. of Urdu, A.M.U., Aligarh.
20. Prof. Surayya Husain: Yaldaram Aazadi-e-Niswan ke aik Alambardar, p-52, Majmooa-e-Maqalat-e-Yaldaram – Seminar 1981, Dept. of Urdu, A.M.U.
21. Colonal G.F.I. Graham: The Life and Works of Sir Syed Ahmad Khan, Willaim Blackwood, London-1885.
22. Sir Syed Ahmad Khan: Musafiran-e-London, p-124. Aligarh Muslim University Old Boys' Association, Karachi-1996.

23. Sir Syed Ahmad Khan: Musafiran-e-London.
24. ibid.
25. Tahzeebul-Akhlaq, vol-3, No:1, p-3.
26. Nafees Bano: Tahzeebul Akhlaq—Tahqiqui wa Tanquidi Mutala, p-125, Nishat Offset Press, Tanda, Faizabad-1993.
27. Prof. Surayya Husain: Sir Syed and Women's Education-"Khwabon ka Sawera."—2004-05.
28. Addresses and Speeches MAO College (1875-1919) p9.
29. Iftikhar Aalam: *Sir Syed Duroon-e-Khana*, p-144, Educational Book House, Aligarh-2006.
30. Akhbar Scientific Society, p-22, Dtd. January 12, 1877.
31. Iftikhar Aalam: Sir Syed Duroon-e-Khana, p-174, Educational Book House, Aligarh.
32. ibid, p-220.
33. Tehzibul Akhlaq, Urdu monthly, Aligarh.
34. Sir Raza Ali: Aamal Namah, p-171, Khuda Bakhsh Oriental Public Library, Patna-1992.
35. S. K. Bhatnagar: History of M.A.O. College, p-355, Asia Publishing House, Bombay-1969.
36. S. K. Bhatnagar: History of M.A.O. College, p-355, Asia Publishing House, Bombay-1969.
37. Rashid Ahmed Siddiqui: Shaikh aur Syed, P-19, Khawateen No—Aligarh Magazine, 2001.
38. Ibid.
39. Shaikh Muhammed Abdullah: *Mushahidat-o-Taassurat*, Female Education Association, Aligarh.
40. Sir Syed ke Lecturon Ka Majmua.
41. Institute Gazette.

42. Sir Syed article 'Aurton kon kis tariqe se Taleem Deni Chahiye?
43. Nafees Bano: Tahzeebul Akhlaq—Tahqiqui wa Tanquidi Mutala, p-243, Nishat Offset Press, Tanda, 1993.
44. Tahzeebul Akhlaq: 15 Shawwal, 1290 A.H.
45. *Mukammil Majmooa Lecture*, p49
46. ibid.
47. Altaf Husain Hali: Hayat-e-Javaid.
48. Altaf Husain Hali: Hayat-e-Javaid, p. 239-40.
49. Tahzeebul Akhlaq: 5 Jamadi-ul-Awwal, 1288 A.H.

3

Muslim Educational Conference: Struggle for Women's Education

The All India Muslim Educational Conference played a vital role in disseminating modern education among the Indian Muslims. It was the first Muslim NGO of its kind in India established in 1886 by the great visionary of the 19th century, Sir Syed Ahmad Khan.

Aligarh was chosen the permanent headquarter of the conference because of Sir Syed and the MAO College which embodied his mission. Its annual meetings were held at different parts of the country, and created awareness among the Muslim population about the significance of modern education.

The contribution of the All India Muslim Educational Conference cannot be overemphasised in pre-Partition days. Apart from the Aligarh Muslim University, the foundation of

Osmania University, Dacca University, Jamia Millia University, Anjuman-i-Taraqqi Urdu, Nadvat-ul-Ulema, Lucknow, Darul Musannafin, Azamgarh etc. owe their growth directly or indirectly to the ceaseless efforts of the conference.

In the beginning, eight objectives were set by the Conference including the spread of European literature among Muslims, promoting it on large scale and providing opportunities for higher education among Muslims, making a probe into the sciences developed by Muslims and making them available for all so that they may be aware of their worth. Making provision for the writing of biographies of renowned Muslim *Ulema* and authors, issuing magazines based on researches of the olden times, and historical accounts or inviting scholars for their illuminating addresses on these topics, training people how to address effectively, making reviews of the religious education in institutions set up by the Muslims for the learning of English language and extending every possible help in that matter.

So far as the services of Muslim Educational Conference regarding women's education are concerned, they are mentioned with golden letters in the pages of history. In the very first Session of Muslim Educational Conference, held on December 27, 1886, presided over by the bosom friend of Sir Syed, Maulvi Muhammad Samiullah Khan Bahadur, at Aligarh, the need to open a branch of the organisation in every village and town was emphasised. Moreover, it was stressed that a census should be conducted in the Muslim dominated areas along with their brief profile. Statistics should also be collected regarding girls' school run by missionaries besides those run by the Government. It would help Muslims to chalk out a concrete plan of future and would enable them to initiate well thought out schemes for Muslim women's educational upliftment.

The third session of Muhammadan Educational Congress was held from December 27 to 29, 1888, at Lahore. The session was convened by the General Secretary of *Anjuman-e-Islam*, Punjab and was presided over by Sardar Muhammad Hayat

Khan. On that occasion, a resolution was proposed for the first time by Shaikh Khairuddin supported by Khalifa Imamuddin, the District Inspector of Schools. In the resolution, it was said: "Muhammadan Educational Congress approves of the plan that Muslims start schools for girls' education which should be as per the teachings of Islam." About one thousand and four hundred delegates attended the gathering, including 288 members of the Conference, especially, Sir Syed Ahmad Khan, Mr. Theodore Beck, the Principal of Madrasatul Uloom, Aligarh; Muhammad Ikramullah Khan; Raja Jahandad Khan; Khwaja Zahoor Ahmad Shah; Shaikh Muhammad Shah; Hafiz Ghulam Muhiuddin, Wakeel—*Anjuman Himayat-e-Islam*, Lahore; Muhammed Hasan Khan, Victoria Jubilee School, Jhang; Munshi Shamsuddin and Syed Meer Hasan.

It was on this historic occasion when Shaikh Muhammad Abdullah saw Sir Syed Ahmad Khan for the first time. He had accompanied his teacher Hakim Maulana Nooruddin to this function. He was moved so much by Sir Syed's movement that he got admission at Aligarh. Now, he is known as the pioneer who launched Muslim women's education in north India.

The sixth Session of All India Muslim Educational Conference was held in 1891 at Aligarh. Convened by Sir Syed Ahmad Khan, it was presided over by Nawab Muhammad Ishaq Khan, son of Nawab Mustafa Khan Shaifta, a close friend of Mirza Ghalib, a world-famous Urdu poet. In this Session as well, the second resolution pertained to female education. It was proposed by Khwaja Ghulam-us-Saqalain and was supported by Justice Maulvi Syed Karamat Husain, who was the founder of Karamat Husain Degree College, Lucknow. The resolution read: "It is essential that women's education should also be taken note of besides that of boys'. The real progress of a community depends on them to a greater part. Their education should be helpful in their moral, educational and religious progress so that they may lead the coming generations on the path of prosperity and goodness."

After return from England, Syed Karamat Husain (1854-1917) was appointed the first Professor of Law at MAO College, Aligarh and worked tirelessly for the cause of women's education in India. He became the member of the Muslim Educational Conference, proposing its first resolution in favour of women's education at its 1891 meeting in Aligarh. He was also instrumental in establishing the women's education section of the Muslim Educational Conference in 1896, headed by Syed Mumtaz Ali until 1902, when Shaikh Abdullah took over the position. In the late 1890s as well, Karamat Husain helped found the Crosthwaite Girl's School in Allahabad.

In 1899, the All India Muhammdan Anglo-Oriental Educational Conference was held at Calcutta and was presided over by Hon'ble Justice Syed Ameer Ali, the Judge of Calcutta High Court. A member of the Rabindera Nath Tagore's family played the host and offered his splendid and spacious place for the venue. The conference was attended by the Lt. Governor of Bengal state, Sir John Woodburn, Maharaja Qasim Bazar, Mr. T. M. Ghosh, Justice Gurudas Benarjee, Mr. Canady, Commissioner of Burdwan, Mr. Danik, Magistrate of Hawrah and Col. Sardar Muhammad Ismail Khan, Ambassador of Kabul. Besides, Nizam of Hyderabad, Meer Mahboob Ali Khan also attended the conference. The trustees of *Madrasatul Uloom* also thanked Mr. Mahboob Ali Khan for his cooperation in the development of the Madrasa. These trustees met Mr. Mahhoob Ali Khan under the leadership of Nawab Mohsin-ul-Mulk, a close associate of Sir Syed.

The Conference in Calcutta became all the more important when a separate wing for women's education was inaugurated there. A resolution was passed with regard to forming state-level committees for the promotion of women's education. The draft resolution read: "The Conference approves of the idea of opening schools for ladies, strictly based on the Islamic rulings and conventions in every state capital. This important job must be done starting from the 1st of January, 1900 upto three years. There should also be established by provincial committees in other states to look after the progress of girls' schools. The syllabus in these schools should be prepared in consultation with reputed *Ulama* of the area concerned." The resolution was tabled by Khan Bahadur Shujaat Ali Baig and supported by Nawab Muhsin-ul -Mulk.

The fourteenth Session of the Conference was convened at Rampur in 1900, presided over by Nawab Imadul Mulk Bahadur, Maulvi Syed Husain Saheb Bilgarami. In this Session, a resolution was proposed by Chaudhary Khushi Muhammad Khan in favour of female education. This was seconded by Aftab Ahmad Khan and supported by the President, who contended that abilities of girls were equal to the boys, and it was therefore most unfair to deny them educational facilities.

The fifteenth Session of the Conference was held in 1901 at the most developed state of south India; Madras (now called Chennai). Justice Boddam of Madras High Court presided over it. This resolution was passed: "To strengthen the cause of women's education among the Muslims of the state, it is necessary that Hobart Girls' High School be recognized and other school started to meet the requirements of the northern portion of the city. The resolution was put by Meer Sultan Muhiuddin and was backed by Maulvi Fakhruddin.

In the Session, convened on February 3, 1902 in Delhi, the number of participants reached 10,361 whereas that of visitors, 310. The Session was presided over by Sir Agha Sultan Mohd. Shah Khan. It was for the first time that a significant number of Europeans attended the function. They included Sir Micheal Backs, Finance Minister of England; Lord Sambrook, Member of Parliament; Sir M. M. Bahao Nagri, M.P., Lord Kachnor, Commander-in-Chief, Indian Armed Forces; Governors of Bombay and Madras; Lt. Governors of United States...and besides Punjab, ladies from England. It was on this very occasion that

Shaikh Muhammed Abdullah was elected Secretary of the wing of Women's Education. In his presidential address Sir Agha Khan III said that one of the main causes of our present apathy is the terrible position of Muslim Women due to *Zanana* and *Pardah* system. There is absolutely nothing in Islam or the Koran or the example of the first two centuries, to justify this terrible and cancerous growth that has for nearly a thousand year eaten into the very vitals of Islamic society.

The Session of 1903 proved to be of great advantage in respect of women's education. Held at the huge and beautiful lawn of *Anjumen-e-Islam*, Bombay, the Session was presided over by Justice Badruddin Tayyabji of the Bombay High Court.

Badruddin Tayyabji as the first Indian barrister in Bombay mixed professionally almost entirely with Europeans. He first encouraged his wife to introduce Zanana parties made up of ladies of various communities. Then she learned some English and began meeting European women. The distinction of first discarding the veil altogether went, however, to one of Judge's niece, Mrs. Ali Akbar Faizi who went to England in 1894. Then in 1898 another niece, Mrs. Hyderi followed suit in Bombay itself at a party given by the Parsi, Jamshedji Tata. As a pioneer of modernization and westernization, Badruddin Tayyabji presented a spirited attack on *Purdah* and early marriage in Bombay at the Mohammadan Educational Conference in 1903.

While presiding over the seventh session at Mumbai, a noted jurist, Badruddin Tayabji pointed out: "Let us just consider for a moment what the absence of 'female education' means. It means in the first place that at least one half of our community is, and must for ever remain, uneducated, illiterate, unenlightened and backward. Is it not obvious that when our mothers, our wives, our daughters, our sisters are uneducated, then our own education must necessarily be of a very imperfect character, and that we must be moving in a dark and unwholesome atmosphere?

How can we hope to have our children brought up and educated, when their mothers are ignorant and illiterate? How can we hope to have high moral principles inculcated when the children move among women who have been never benefited by high moral and intellectual training?

The third resolution was moved for Women's education which aimed at 'popularising education among the Muslim ladies'. The star speakers who addressed the distinguished gathering were Nawab Muhsin-ul- Mulk; Allama Nazeer Ahmad; Allama Shibli Nomani; Maulana Altaf Husain Hali and Maulana Syed Shah Sulaimn Phulwari-all top religious leaders of the country. In the entire history of Muslim Educational Conference, women also got the opportunity to attend and experience the proceedings of the Conference for the first time from behind the screen. On this occasion, an educational exhibition was held consisting of maps, pictures, photographs, globes and handmade objects prepared by women. People showed immense interest as it was the first exhibition of its own kind organized by the Muslims. The Governor of Bombay, Lord Willingdon made special mention of the exhibition in his address. The representatives or the delegates saw the kindergarten system of education. Muslims of India had never seen or heard about such a system before. For this, arrangements were made at *Anjuman-e-Islam* school. Consensus was also obtained on this occasion regarding the establishment of Teacher Training Schools to prepare Muslim lady teachers for the instruction of SGG.

At this session, Shaikh Abdullah said: "I had the first opportunity to be introduced to the educated women form Bombay. Of them, three were the daughters of Late Justice Badruddin Tayyabji and two of them were the Faizi Saheb's daughters, namely, Zohra Faizi and Atiya Faizi. Besides, there were some two or three ladies from the educated families of Bombay."

The year 1904 proved to be a milestone in the movement of Muslim women's education. Shaikh Muhammad Abdullah issued a magazine, *Khatoon* the same year under his editorship. That very year, the 18th Session of All India Muslim Educational Conference was held at Lucknow and presided over by the Principal of M.A.O. College, Theodore Morrison. For the first time, the cause of women's education was approved and patronised by the state. The Session on female education was presided over by Shah Deen, a barrister from Lahore. A resolution was passed to establish a girls' school at Aligarh. Raja Tasadduq Rasool Khan of Jhangirabad, Raja Sir Mohammad Ali Mohammad Khan of Mahmoodabad, Shaikh Iltifat Rasool of Sandila, Nawab Saifuddin Husam-ul Mulk Maulvi Syed Ali Hasan Khan, Raja Naushad Ali Khan, Munshi Ahtisham Ali Khan, Mr. Mohammad Nasim, Advocate of Lucknow, Mr. Mohammad Rafiq, Mr. Shahid Husain, Talaqedar Gaddia (District Pratapgarh), Mr. Mohammad Ali, B.A. (Oxen), Nawab Mohsin-ul-Mulk , Khwaja Ghulam-us-Saqlain etc. participated.

The Session started with the happy news announced by the Secretary of the Conference, Nawab Muhsin-ul- Mulk, that Nawab Sultan Jahan, ruler of Bhopal had sanctionred a grant to the Aligarh College for women's education. The grant consisted of Rs. 34,000/- (thirty-four thousand rupees). Thus, the total collection made for the first time for women's education amounted to Rs. 44,250/- (forty-four thousand, two hundred and fifty rupees). "Sheikh Abdullah and his wife organized an exhibition of handicrafts by Muslim women and held a meeting of educated Muslim women from all over the country, as ways of calling attention to the talents and educational needs of the women of their community".

After the death of Nawab Muhsin-ul -Mulk, Nawab Viquar-ul- Mulk became the Secretary of the All India Muslim Educational Conference. He convened the Session in 1907 at Madrasa Islamia, Karachi, presided over by a well-known Urdu poet and biographer of Sir Syed, Khwaja Altaf Husain Hali. In his inaugural address, Hali threw light on the educational backwardness of Muslims of Sindh and presented some statistics. He also read out a very effective poem on the condition of Muslims:

Zamana naam hai mera to mein sabko dikha doonga,

Ki jo taaleem se bhagenge, naam unke mita doonga.

(O man! My name is Time. I order you to get education, otherwise you'll perish and no one will ever make mention of yours).

The dignitaries who attended this Session included Nawab Viqarul Mulk, and Syed Muhammad Husain (Chief Minister of Patiala State). A leading businessman from Bombay Sir Adamji Peer Bhoy (ex-sherrif of Bombay), Justice Shah Deen, Major Syed Hasan Bilgrami and Mr. Ali Imam, Barrister were also present. A resolution was passed on this occasion to prepare a syllabus based on religious and moral values for the Muslim boys and girls for Sindh.

The president of the session, Khwaja Altaf Husain Hali (1837-1914) served the British as an educator and translator and supporter of female education. In 1874, he published Majalis-un-Nissa (Assemblies of women), fictionalized conversations among women in a prosperous, urban Muslim household. The women discuss their daily routine and emphasize the necessity for women to be educated in order to mange their households, raise their children, establish proper relations with all the members and servants in their families, and to be the understanding companions to their husbands.

The twenty- third Session was held in Rangoon (Yangon), capital of Burma (Myanmar) in 1909 and was presided over by Raja of Mahmoodabad, Sir Mohammad Ali Mohammed Khan. The Conference was attended by two hundred and fifty delegates all the way from the Punjab, Bengal, Bihar Madras, Bombay, Hyderabad and Assam. These dignitaries travelled either by air or ship. On this occasion, the Lt. Governor of Burma, Sir Herbert White announced that his government would try to implement the proposed recommendations which will benefit the Muslims of Burma.

Sir Mohammad Ali Mohammad Khan, Raja of Mahmoodabad said: "We want Aligarh to be such a home of learning as to command the same respect of scholars as Berlin or Oxford, Leipzig or Paris. And we want those branches of Muslim learning which are in the midst of decay, to be enriched by Muslim scholars to be stock of the world's knowledge."

On this occasion the wife of Lieutinent Governor, Mrs. White inaugurated the All India Ladies' Art Exhibition at the Rangoon College Hall amidst a very large and influential assembly, the organization of which was done by Mr. Abdullah. Over 550 exhibits were catalogued; some of the best among whom being these sent in by Her Highness, the Maharani of Bhavanagar who was conferred with a gold medal. Mrs. M. Laurie, the daughter of the Lieutinat –Governor also grace the exhibition.

The twenty-fourth Session was held at Nagpur on December 29-30, 1910, presided over by Allama Abdullah Ibn Yusuf Ali, a Cambridge graduate and Principal of Islamia College, Lahore. In his presidential address, he said, "The equality between men and women is prerequisite for the civilizational growth if only the benefit of man is to be talked about. The progress of our brethrens as well as our coming generations depends on the fact that our mothers, sisters, wives and daughters should be at least equal to us in education and experience of life if not more advanced than us."

The next session was called on December 4, 1911 on the occasion of crowning ceremony in Delhi. It was presided over by Nawab Imadul Mulk Bahadur Maulvi Syed Husain Saheb Bilgarami. Nawab Sultan Jahan Begum presided over the Women's Education Session. It was for the first time in the history of Indian Muslims that rulers of a country participated with the common men in a public gathering to discuss public issues.

In 1912, another programme was organised at Qaiser Bagh, Baradari, Lucknow under the presidentship of Major Syed Hasan Bilgarami. This time also, an exhibition based on women-made handicrafts was held, inaugurated by the wife of Lt. Governor Sir James Meston.

The twenty-seventh Session of the All India Muslim Educational Conference was held at Agra in the year 1913 under the chairmanship of the Judge of Lahore High Court, Sir Shah Din (1868-1918). Emphasising the importance of women's education, Justice Shah Din said in his presidential address: "No scheme of national education will be complete among the Indian Mohammadans which does not make ample provision for the education of women on modern lines, with special reference to the particular needs of a progressive Islamic community. This does not by any means imply the wholesome adoption of the methods of instruction and of the standard of culture which have come to be associated with western civilization. We in East have our own distinctive traditions and predominant tendencies of thought, and we must evolve a new type of culture as the result of the wholesome combination of the Asiatic and European systems of training. One thing is, however, clear, and that is that the purely Eastern modes of education would be as stale, insipid and unprofitable in the case of our women as they have proved to be in the case of our own men, and the community must make its mind once and for all to allow its girls to be instructed in the elements of knowledge according to the more scientific methods of the modern age". The time was long since gone by when even our leading men forward the idea of concentrating all our energies upon perfecting the education of boys before taking up the question of educating our girls; we have advanced far beyond the stage at which such a view could be held and acted upon without endangering our national position in India"

The twenty-eighth Session was held in Rawalpindi in 1914. In his presidential address, Janab Maulvi Sir Rahim Bakhsh, President Council, Bhawalpur believed that women too should be educated side by side with men. Homes, which are the nurseries of children who grow up into men and women, will be good or bad according to the power that governs them is the mother. The first great instructor is the example of the mother that is constantly held up before the child and influences its whole course of life. In the respective and deeply impressionable and initiative period of growth the model that is daily moulding in the nature of the child is the mother. It is, I hope, not saying too much that the happiness or misery, enlightenment or ignorance, the temper, the disposition, the likes or the dislikes with which young men grow up, depend, in a very great measure, upon the exercise of women's power in her special kingdom of home.

Women, for better or for worse, in our zeal and our woe, are our co-partners of life, and such being the case, I think it is a religious, a moral and a social obligation that we should educate them, and make worthy to be our comrades and co-partners in life".

A Session was called on the invitation of the Prime Minister of Khairpur, Khan Bahadur Sindh, Shaikh Sadiq Ali in 1919. The arrangements were made by the Minister of Khairpur, Khan Bahadur Maulvi Muhammad Ibrahim and Maulvi Sir Rahim Bakhsh; President Council Bhawalpur presided over it. Mr. Muhammad Ayyub Khan was also present in the function who became the President of Pakistan. In this programme, demands were made of the Government to make necessary arrangements regarding the education of Muslim girls for Sindh; it was also decided that a committee should be formed based on the educated people for the education of Muslim girls. It was also demanded that more scholarships be sanctioned for Muslim lady teachers.

After the establishment of the Aligarh Muslim University in 1920, it was also decided to convene the Session of All India Muslim Educational Conference in 1922 on the occasion of the first Annual Convocation. The Session was presided over by the Education Minister of the Punjab, Khan Bahadur Sir Mian Fazal-i-Husain. Nawab Muzammilullah Khan was appointed the Chief of the Reception Committee. A large number of educationists from all parts of the country participated in it. Speeches of Maulana Syed Sulaiman Nadvi and Dr. Sir Shafat Ahmad Khan were particularly given big hands.

On this occasion, Shaikh Muhammad Abdullah offered an important proposal regarding women's education which was backed by the Nawab of Meerut, Mahmood Ali Khan. In it "the need for compulsory education of girls" was brought home. For those Muslim families where veil was not observed, it was emphasised that girls should attend school. At the same time, stress was laid that girls of veil-observing families should also attend school upto the age of ten and for them arrangements for conveyance was recommended. It was for the first time that suggestions were made to educate the girls.

Besides, consensus was also reached to start a Teachers' Training College and an Engineering College at Aligarh Muslim University.

The 1923-Session was also convened at Aligarh under the Presidentship of Sahibzadah Aftab Ahmad Khan (1867-1930), an active member of Muslim Educational Conference and the Vice-Chancellor of Aligarh Muslim University. Sahibzada Aftab Ahmad Khan belonged to the first generation of Aligarh. On female education, he lamented that the objective of female education should be not merely to produce good wives and mothers but to develop and train to the full brains and bodies of the "better half" of the population. If the brains and bodies of the "better half" are undeveloped and untrained, how can the national stock of our spiritual, mental, moral and physical wealth come up to the standards of those nations and countries where the best possible educational facilities are provided for every individual, whether male or female. It is therefore essential that we should have a correct idea as to the nature and scope of this great subject".

Our female education and training should be designed, so far as possible, to implement, in the minds and character of our girls the spirit on the following verse in the holy Quran:

> "O Prophet! Say to your wives. If you desire this world's life and its ornaments, then come, I will give you a provision and allow you to depart dodily. And

> if you desire Allah and His Apostle and the latter, abode, then surely Allah has prepared for the doers of good among you a mighty reward."

An educational exhibition was also held on this occasion and every aspect of life was taken into consideration. Models, pictures and maps concerning the birth of a child and the safety of the lying-in mother were provided in the Mushtaq Manzil. A lady doctor explained the points with the help of pictures. Thus, the awareness about women's education grew. On the one hand, women were allowed to take part in the Bombay Session from behind the screens, topics like health care had begun attracting the attention of Muslims. These changes were indicative of some great revolution.

In this exhibition, equipment which had been invented to solve the problems of physics and astronomy was also presented besides scouting, football, tennis, cricket and hockey. In India, it was the first exhibition of its kind dealing with education. A majority of the articles put at the show were those brought from England by Sahibzadah Aftab Ahmad Khan.

In 1924, the Session was called at Bombay Globe Cinema Hall, situated on the Sandherst Road at the request of a renowned barrister of India, Mr. Muhammad Ali Jinnah (who later on came to be known as Qaid-e-Azam and founder of Pakistan). Lodging arrangements were made at the Apolo and Taj Mahal hotels for the guests. Two public meetings were also organised consisting of five thousand people. On this occasion, Mr. M.C. Chhagla (ex-Education Minister of India), Maulvi Rafiuddin (barrister of Poona) and Mr. Ziauddin Barni, etc., also made some proposals. For the first time, a demand was made to make provisions for Muslim girl students to appear in the examinations of higher studies privately at the Bombay and other national universities. Aligarh Muslim University enforced this resolution first of all. Even today, girl candidates can appear privately in the examinations.

Under the presidentship of ex-Judge of Madras High Court, Sir Abdur Rahim, the thirty ninth session was held at Delhi in 1926. The Conference had already convened three Sessions in Delhi before this one.

On this occasion, Maulvi Syed Tufail Ahmad Manglori put a demand to open a Pardah Primary School in a locality based on more than two thousand population. Dr. Sir Shafat Ahmad Khan supported it. Another important resolution was passed on this occasion. The resolution said that traditional veil system of India is an obstacle in the progress of women, to which Hakim Muhammad Ajmal Khan from Nadvatul Ulema had referred in the Kanpur Session. Therefore, the Conference requested the respected *Ulema* to take note of the point of the President and make provisions in the light of *Shariat* so that women may go outside their houses wearing the burqa and girls may get education. This resolution was the brainchild of Syed Ahmad Kazmi, a lawyer from Saharanpur, whereas Maulvi Mahmood Ahmad Abbas supported it.

While tabling the proposal, Syed Ahmad Kazmi said, "Women cannot be educated as long as the un-Islamic practice of veiling continues; and unless women are educated, men's education will suffer. Therefore, the traditional veiling should be substituted with the Islamic one, practised in the Islamic countries.

The fortieth Muslim Educational Conference Session was held in 1927 which was presided over by one of the active participants of the Aligarh Movement, Sir Shaikh Abdul Qadir. The venue was Madras for the second time. In this Session, a large number of women also participated. Dr. Mukhtar Ahmad Ansari, President Indian National Congress; Sir Ibrahim Rahmatullah, President Indian Industrial Commercial Congress; Mr. Natrajan, President Indian Social Conference were also present. The session on Women's Education and Civilization was presided over by Justice Sir Shah Sulaiman, Judge of Allahabad High Court. Seven resolutions regarding the education of Muslim women were passed. In the history of the Conference, so many resolutions on the education of Muslim girls had never been passed. In this way, education of Muslim girls became part of the agenda of Muslims.

Delivering the presidential address, Sir Shaikh Abdul Qadir observed: " No nation can rise to its full stature unless the female portion of its population is highly developed intellectually as well as physically. The education of girls in India has been very much neglected for years past and much more so among the Muslims".

He further said: "I may add just a world before passing on the something else and that is with reference to the change brought about by the existing political reforms, under which women have been given the right to vote at the elections for the various legislative bodies in India. If you desire that the privilege thus extended to them may be utilized and they may be able to take their proper share in the councils of their country, you can not but adopt a vigorous policy of female education and must incur much larger expenditure on its then you have so far done."

In 1927, the leadership recognized the need for Muslim female education in the universities and colleges. Simultaneously, the principle of force and compulsory secondary education for all Muslim girls was accepted, and the government was urged to provide free lunch and transport to economically disadvantaged girls.

That Muslim Head Mistress, holding certificate, should be appointed in Muslim Girls' Schools to promote women's education among Muslims was approved by the delegates.

In 1928, the Session of the Conference was held at the Osmania Hall, Islamia Moinia High School in Ajmer under the chairmanship of Justice Sir Shah Muhammad Sulaiman, Judge of Allahabad High Court. Rai Bahdur Seth Teekam Chand offered his vast mansion for the guests. In this Session, delegates were also present from Mysore University, University of Dhaka (Dacca) and Osmania University, Hyderabad.

Highlighting the importance of female education, Sir Shah Mohammad Sulaiman said that "the country demands the education of the entire population for the growth of national consciousness, and a spirit of self-reliance. Mass education is a requirement of the most vital importance if India is to advance in the scale of civilization. And that progress has to be an all round one and irrespective of sex.

Higher education for female has to be on the same lines as the higher education for boys. It can be meant only for those highly advanced ladies who desire to make an independent earning like men. The Purdah system in the rigid form in which it prevails among Muslims is a serious difficulty in their way, but not necessarily an insuperable one.

Considerable facilities exist for acquiring education with due regard to Purdah. There are many well-equipped girls' schools and women's colleges which are reserved for females exclusively. For those who wish to acquire a high education the doors of such institutions are always open."

A demand of two lakh rupees was made from the Rajasthan Government for the promotion of women's education besides establishing a full fledged Muslim Girls' School, taking into consideration the increasing number of Muslim girls in the state. Also, an appeal was made to the Nawab of Tonk to fix the educational budget at 10 per cent to remove illiteracy from the area and to make sufficient arrangements for women's education.

The most backward area in terms of uneducated Muslims was Rohtak, where a Session was convened in 1931, presided over by Syed Raza Ali, Nawab of Rampur. At that time, not ten out of the vast population of Muslims constituting to about one and a half lakh were not educated in the district of Rohtak. The irony is that Rohtak used to be a centre of learning in the past, and was inhabited first of all by the forefathers of Hazrat Shah Waliullah Muhaddith Dehlavi .

On this occasion, the resolution regarding women's education was proposed by the Vice-Principal of Arabic College, Delhi, Shaukat Husain Zaidi. The resolution was supported by the great scholar of Islam and the Imam of Jama Masjid, Delhi Hazarat Maulvi Syed Ahmad. He was the father of ex-Imam of Shahi Jama Masjid, Delhi, Maulana Syed Abdullah Bukhari. In this Conference, Muslims were requested to grant scholarships to educate women in large numbers. It was also stressed that Muslim teachers be appointed in large numbers. As for the religious and moral education of women, suggestions were made to assign the task to the lady Muslim teachers.

Thereafter, the Session was called at Lahore in 1932 under the presidentship of the Col Maqbool Hasan Quraishi, Education Minister of the Bhawalpur state. For the first time, a lady Principal Khadija Begum, M.A. was included on the board of members, was given the task of preparing the syllabus of girls' education. Demands were made to reserve fifty per cent quota for Muslim staff in Government and Board schools and to appoint Muslim Principal in Muslim dominated districts, taking into consideration the educational backwardness of Muslim girls. At the same time, it was also demanded that Urdu language be a compulsory subject in all Government schools. These demands were made by Khawaja Gul Muhammad Advocate from Firozpur which was supported by the Principal, Mushtaq Ahmad Zahidi from Bhawalpur (now in Pakistan).

The conference demanded the appointment of Muslim female faculty members at all government colleges and universities. The Muslim leadership changed its traditional orientation for female education rather slowly, and did not recognize the principle of equality in modern education until 1930s.

The next Session was called at the vast ground of Faiz-e-Aam Inter College, Meerut on March 31, 1934, presided over by Nawab Muzammilullah Khan Shervani. The reception committee was headed by Nawab Ismail Khan, who was also appointed the

Vice Chancellor of Aligarh Muslim University in later years. The vice-president of the welcome committee was Bhayya Shaikh Bashiruddin; and secretary, Khan Bahadur Muhammad Aslam Saifi (an illustrious son of Maulvi Ismail Meeruthi). As Shaikh Abdullah was called Papa Mian and his wife, Begum Waheed Jahan was called Aala Bi; similarly Aslam Saifi and his wife were called Abbaji and Ammaji respectively. Ismail Meeruti, father of Aslam Saifi, established the first institute for Muslim girls' education in the north India, which is still extant and known as Ismail Girls Inter College and Degree College. Ismail Meeruti was a close friend of Sir Syed. He had played a key role in formulating the syllabus of M.A.O. College. Meerut also has the credit of playing a lead role in creating awareness among women. The disciple of Mirza Ghalib, Hakeem Muhammad Faseehuddin Ranj Meeruti wrote the first book in 1861 on poetesses, which should be regarded as the first document of educational awareness among women.

Incidentally, the first resolution regarding the establishment of Women's College at Aligarh Muslim University was moved in the Meerut session. On this occasion, Khan Bahadur Muhammad Aslam Saifi said, "The Conference deems it vitally essential to start a Girls' College at Aligarh for providing higher education. More importantly, arrangements should be made for the studies of graduation level in the existing Intermediate Girls' College. For this purpose, money will be required. Therefore, the Conference appeals the community for cooperation." Among the dignitaries who attended the Session, special mention may be made of Sir Ross Masud (a grandson of Sir Syed), Vice Chancellor of Muslim University; Nawab Sadaryar Jang Maulvi Habibur Rahman Khan Sherwani; Baba-e-Urdu Maulvi Abdul Haq; Khan Bahadur Maulavi Bashiruddin, editor Al-Bashir (Etawah); Hafiz Hidayat Husain, Barrister at law; Maulana Hafiz Ahmad Saeed Dehlavi; Maulana Hifzur Rahman Seoharvi; Hafeez Jalandhari and Abdul Azeez Advocate from Allahabad.

On February 21, 1936, the Conference convened its three-day Session at Rampur on the invitation of Nawab of Rampur, Sir Muhammad Raza Ali Khan. It was presided over by Sir Sultan Muhammad Shah Agha Khan. The Session on woman's education was presided over by Nawabzada Liaqat Ali Khan, Bar-at-law, who was elected the Prime Minister of Pakistan after the Partition of India.

On this occasion, four resolutions were passed:

1. Since girls are getting education at girls' schools and colleges, they are getting detached from Islamic teachings and civilization. That is the reason people are not attracted towards women's education. Therefore, the conference decided to "prepare such a syllabus for them as is strictly in accordance with the Islamic teachings."
2. Taking into consideration the lack of Muslim lady teachers, the Conference decided the "scholarships to poor girls of High School be sanctioned for education at college or the Training College on the condition that after the completion of education they will teach in girls' schools."
3. In the third resolution, it was said that considering the acute lack of women's education in Muslims in India, the Conference decided to adopt well-thought out strategy to make the cause of women's education a success; and to earmark a part of the aid granted to national schools by the Conference for girls' schools.
4. The fourth and last resolution was based on the fact that due to pressing needs, Muslim Girls' College must be upgraded to the Degree College; and B.A. classes must be started from the Academic Session beginning after summer vacations.

The fifty-first Session of All India Muslim Educational Conference was held on December 29, 1940 at Poona. It was presided over by the Prime Minister of Bengal, Sir A. K. Fazlul Haq. President of the welcome committee, Ahmad Ibraheem Haroon Jafar said in his welcome address, "The backwardness of education among Muslim girls is the most damaging blot on the prestige of the community. It has been said that in educating a man, we educate an individual but in educating a woman we educate a family. Our community stands in sore need of educated women who will give a lead to their sisters in respect of education. A community, whose women folk are illiterate, can never prosper and will always lag behind, while other communities which have realized the importance of education, and take steps to make provision for it, are all on the way of prosperity.

We must formulate immediate measures for removing the causes underlying this problem. Some of these are pardah, public opinion against female education, public opinion against co-education, poverty and want of qualified or trained female Muslim teachers. The last factor constitutes the most serious problem affecting the progress of education among the Muslims. Unless serious attempts are made to secure teacher and overcome public prejudices, not much will be achieved in this direction.

With the dawn of independence on the horizon of India, this organisation, too, became independent of its responsibilities to a considerable extant. It became as though devoid of any vigour, whereas its branch *Ajuman Taraqqui Urdu-e- Hind* is still at work for the promotion of Urdu language. Not only that, it has been rendering valuable services by way of the publication of Urdu books since the time the branch made Delhi its head quarters.

Shaikh Muhammad Abdullah, one of the active members of All India Muslim Educational Conference, expressed his view about the Conference in his autobiography, "*Mushahidat-o-Taassurat*". 'Unfortunately, the Conference has lost its vigour. No signs of vitality are to be seen despite the fact that it has enjoyed a glorious past. Nawab Mohsin-ul-Mulk had nurtured it with great care along with Sahibzada Aftab Ahmad Khan. Late Sahibzada had arranged a big sum of money as a gift from Nawab Sultan Jahan Begum and spent on the Conference's office, constructed after Sultan Jahan. The building is still extant and houses the office of the Conference.'

Shaikh Sahib further writes about the role of the management of the Conference. "Their state is no better now than those in the service of a Saint's Tomb who informs people, visiting to the place, about the achievement and lineage of the pious soul resting inside the grave and relate the area under their possession to the remembering of the deceased. I am deeply grieved to see the degradation of the splendid edifice — the same edifice which was the fruition of tremendous efforts of Sahibzada Aftab Ahmad Khan. Though the Conference still breathes, but it can properly be likened to a premature death."

General Secretary of the All India Muslim Educational Conference, Prof. Riazur Rahman Khan Sherwani has also made mention of the degradation in the 57th Session, held at Delhi in 1993. The 56th Session of the Conference was held in Madras in 1955, presided over by Dr. Zakir Husain. He said, "It's sad that since 1953, no Session has so far been held ...that's to say, no annual Session for thirty-eight years and no general meeting for fifteen years."

Addressing the 57th annual Session of the Conference at Ghalib Academy, New Delhi, on October 24, 1993, Mr. Sayied Hamid, former Vice Chancellor of the Aligarh Muslim University, discussed the state of inaction in these words, "So for as Muslim Educational Conference is concerned, its motto was to introduce the Aligarh Movement in every house across the country. In the initial period, it worked wonders. Later on, it started focusing on all the major issues, pertaining to Muslims. The Conference also dealt with politics. And this is the key factor behind the low-performance of the Conference in the field of education in my humble view. Till 1920, the Conference worked with full vigour without doubt.

With the establishment of the Aligarh Muslim University, the Conference surrendered itself, as if it were of no relevance any more. This surrender was deliberate or not, I cannot say. What I have to say is that there is no activity going on in the Conference for the past sixty years and for the past half a century, it has become as useless as an appendix, attached to the lower end of the large intestine. A poet has said that carelessness of a moment (sometimes) is to be paid for centuries.

What to say of a moment, complete fifty years have lapsed but no action took place. Mention many be made of the Conference, organised by Syed Gohar Wala. Muslims from the south kept looking at it for a long time after Independence hoping that it would lead them in the cause of education. About thirty years back or so, they detached themselves from the Conference because of the latter's poor performance, and started their own movement. Muslim Education Society was established at Kerala (by the Old Boys of Aligarh Muslim University); Al-Ameen Society at Karnataka; and S.I.T. at Tamil Nadu. They all worked well and won appreciation. In Andhra Pradesh, especially at Hyderabad, active associations and institutions mushroomed. Therefore, there is no ray of hope that the revival of the Aligarh Movement will take place at Aligarh. Now, the concentration has drifted towards the south. If the Aligarh Movement ever regains its vigour, it would cover the north India at the most."

The Honorary Joint Secretary of the Conference and the former Principal of Islamia College, Etawah, Mr. Amanullah Khan Sherwani wrote, "The vast institution has now been transformed into an office, entrusted to the task of collecting monthly rent from some houses and shops and getting salaries. For name's sake, little grant is given to few Madrasas and a little financial aid to some poor and needy students. In the 1988-89 Budget, only five thousand rupees were earmarked under these heads, but the expenditure did not exceed too few hundreds."

The Parliament of India has made five of conference members the right of being a part of the University Court under the Amendment Act of 1981 of the University in recognition of the historical significance and contribution of the Conference.

Days are gone when there was all around opposition to Sir Syed. Muslims are increasingly inching towards institution-building. We do not have Maulvis like Maulavi Imdad Ali to issue *fatwa-e-kufr* (edict of blasphemy). Nor do we have poets like Akbar Allahabadi to make Aligarh Movement an object of criticism and mockery. It is high time that a new breath of vitality is blown into the dormant body of the Conference and, thus, Muslim may again gather under a common banner to meet the modern challenges.

References

1. Altaf Husain Hali: Hayat-e-Javaid, p-203.
2. Panjah Salah (fifty years') Tarikh of All India Muslim Educational Conference: p-4; pub. Nizami Press, Badaun-1937.
3. Khutbate Aaliyah: p-35, Vol.I, by: Anwar Ahmad Marahravi, Muslim University Press, A.M.U. Aligarh-1935.
4. Shaikh Abdullah: Mushahidat-o-Taassurat, p-143-44.
5. Gail Minault: A woman of substance; p xxii, published by Zuban, Hauz Khas, New Delhi
6. Shaikh Abdullah-Mushahidat-o-Tasurat
7. Ibid
8. Khutbat-e-Aliya, Anwar Ahmad Marhervi, Muslim University Press, Aligarh 1935
9. Dr. Rahat Abrar: Ranj Meeruti; p-138, Educational Book House, Shamshad Market, Aligarh.

10. Khutbat-e-Sadarat. Published from Ajmal Press, Bombay-3, p-12.
11. Ruidad-e-Sattavanvan Salana Ijlas by Prof. Riazurrahman Khan Sherwani, p-4.
12. Amaanullah Khan Sherwani: All India Muslim Educational Conference ke Sau Saal, p-190, Office of Muslim Educational Conference, Sultan Jahan Manzil, Aligarh.

In Maharashtra, Justice [illegible] Family gave much [illegible] [illegible] second niece, Begum, [illegible] women and [illegible] fond of western idea[illegible] was against veil [illegible] and, the most educated [illegible]

Maharashtra [illegible] the [illegible] to education [illegible] They faced many hardships [illegible]

4

Shaikh Muhammad Abdullah: a Pioneer of Women's Education

If Sir Syed was the pioneer of modern education among Indian Muslims, Shaikh Muhammad Abdullah was the pioneer of Muslim women's education. The Vice Chancellor of Aligarh Muslim University, Dr. Zakir Husain introduced Shaikh Saheb to the Egyptian Commander-in-Chief, Gen. Najeeb in these words, "Shaikh Saheb is the founder of women's education in our country."

Shaikh Muhammad Abdullah was one of the favourite disciples of the chief exponent of modern ideology and thinking, Sir Syed Ahmad Khan (1817-1898). He was one of the earliest graduates of Muhammadan Anglo-Oriental College, but his greatest contribution is the promotion of modern education among Muslim women. Just as Sir Syed had to undergo severe criticism when he propagated boys' education, Shaikh Abdullah was both physically and emotionally abused when he took the banner of Muslim women's education.

Shaikh Muhammad Abdullah was born on June 21, 1874 in a Brahmin family in Kashmir. His forefather, Pt. Suraj Ram had migrated to the Kashmir from Ayodhya. In Kashmir, his descendents lived at Mohalla Renawari of Srinagar for four generations. Among his descendents was Nikka Ram who left Renawari for Tahseel Khota, district Rawalpindi. The term *'Mehta'* which is a title of honour was used for this family. Nikka Ram's son Bhojder left Naral and settled at Kohistan in Poonch. Here, he established a village after his name, Bhojthan, which later came to be called, Bhantheen and is today known as Bhantani for a long time. To date, the area is under the rule of Bhojder's descendents.

In the fourth generation of Mahta, Bhojder was a God-fearing saint, Mahta Chand, and in popular folk tradition, he was known to perform miracles. Mehta Chand had a brother, named, Mathra whose children flourished and prospered well. In Mathra's third generation, there were four brothers. Of them, Mitha Ram and Kesar Ram had children. Mitha Ram had two sons, viz, Dilbagh Rai and Gharibu. The two brothers joined hands with the grandson of Kesar Ram, Mehta Mast Ram helped Maharaja Gulab Singh extensively during the troubled period of Shamso Rajoli. Thanks to this help, Dogra family got the possession of Poonch. Mehta Mast Ram had two sons: Maher Singh and Gurmukh Singh. The eldest son of Maher Singh, Mehta Roop Singh also ascended the throne.

Mehta Gurmukh Singh had four sons, Thakur Das, Sunder Das, Munshi Hari Singh and Tara Singh. Thakur Das converted to Islam and came to be known as Shaikh Muhammad Abdullah. Mehta Narandra Singh Talwar is a descendent of the family and lives in Poonch and practices law. He himself tells that three brothers among his forefathers, namely, Ghiyana, Mana and Diwana had taken shelter in the valley of Kashmir and had left Ayodhya. The trio saw a vision at the same time. Somebody asked them to lift the stone lying nearby and carry it as far as possible. The point beyond which they fail to carry the stone should be chosen for their residence. In a deserted hill near Poonch, they pitched their tent as per the divine instruction and started worshipping the stone.

Later, the area came to be known as Bhan Tani after the term 'Teen Bhai, which is now part of the PoK. Even today, the family is called Devyal after the name of Deva. One of the forefathers of the family, Mehta Mast Ram converted to Sikhism in the times of battle and became the chief of Gurudwara Nagali Saheb, at Poonch. Prof. Wakil Singh, son of Hari Singh retired from the Department of Physics, Maulana Abul Kalam Azad College, Jammu University. Journalist Mehta Narandra Singh Talwar as one of the grandson of Harbans Singh came to Aligarh along with his uncle and brother-in-law for the first time in February 2007 to attend the centenary celebrations of the Women's College.

Mohammaduddin "Fauq" has made a detailed description of Shaikh Muhammad Abdullah and the lineage in the book, *Tarikh-e-Aqwam-e-Poonch* (Kashmir). He has linked them with the Saraswat Brahmin family.

Thakur Das was very much fond of education since his childhood. His earliest teacher was Qazi Qutbuddin Kashmiri. Later on, he was admitted to the school of Mian Nizamuddin at Poonch. Everyday he used to trek five kilometres to attend the classes in Poonch. During this period, he learned some English from a Bengali Babu and Sanskrit from a Panditji.

In the days when Thakur Das got admitted in Mian Nizamuddin's school, Maharaja Ranbeer Singh appointed an experienced Hakeem (Unani physician), Maulvi Nooruddin as his private physician. Hakeem Sahib lived in Jammu. Once, Maharaja Moti Singh's son Tikka Baldev Singh fell seriously ill. Hakeem was called to Poonch from Jammu. From then on, Hakeem Sahib became a frequent visitor to Poonch. Raja Moti Singh had appointed him as his family physician. A close relationship was also established between Hakeem Nooruddin and the Prime Minister Mian Nizamuddin. Whenever, Hakeem Saheb visited Poonch, he stayed with the Prime Minister. While staying at Poonch, Hakeem Saheb would occasionally visit the school, too, where he came in touch with the student Thakur Das. In the first meeting itself, Thakur Das was deeply impressed with Hakeem Nooruddin and vice versa. But neither of them knew that one day they would become teacher and taught, leading to a great revolution in Thakur Das' life.

Hakeem Maulvi Nooruddin was also a great scholar of Islam besides being a renowned physician. He was well-read in *Fiqh*, *Hadith* and *Tafseer*, and as equally competent in philosophy and physical sciences. When Ghulam Ahmad Qadyani started his movement, he entered his order and after his Guru's death, took his seat. He carried Thakur Das with him to Jammu to give him lessons of *Hikmat* (unani medicine). In Jammu, Maulvi Abdul Karim Sialkoti, a student of Maulvi Nooruddin was also staying at his teacher's house. He taught English to Thakur Das for two to three months and enabled him to be promoted to class Vth. His schoolmasters, viz., Indira Narain and Mukund Lal were very impressed with his intelligence. Thakur Das got a double promotion and was moved to VIII class due to his excellent performance in the annual examination.

Soon, news reached the Maharaja that Hakeem Nooruddin was trying to convert a Hindu boy to Islam. Maharaja Ameer Singh's representative, Diwan Amar Singh, conveyed the message to Thakur Das that he must not go to Maulvi Nooruddin's home in future but stay in the house of Pandit Nand Lal until his father comes to take him home. Despite these orders, Thakur Das continued to meet Hakeem Sahib who was then exiled from the state.

He went home during the summer vacations of 1887 but, instead of returning to Jammu, he went to Lahore to get admission in the Government High School located in the haveli of Raja Dhyan Singh. Hakeem Nooruddin had already informed some people of Thakur Das arrival and asked them to look after him. He continued to visit him in Lahore during intervals.

In 1889, his mentor came to Lahore and took Thakur Das to Ludhiana where Ghulam Ahmad Qadiani called his followers to swear allegiance. In 1890, Thakur Das accompanied Maulvi Sahib to Qadian and accepted his religion, taking the name of Abdullah which means the same as Thakur Das, the 'servant of God'. Now he ate at the same table with his Muslim friends but he did not announce his conversion to his family since he was worried about its effect on his mother and the social repercussions for the family.

During the study period at Aligarh, he had frequent religious skirmishes with his class fellow, Maulana Zafar Ali Khan, who was the Editor of the newspaper, '*Zameendar*', and was a severe critic of the Ahmadiya sect.

After two years, he went to Qadian during the summer vacations in the M.A.O. College and severed his relationship and renounced the discipleship of Mirza Ghulam Ahmad Qadyani.

On the authority of his father's younger brother, Tara Singh, Mohsin Abdullah says, "When one of his family-members, Thakur Das embraced Islam, the Madrasa of Poonch, where Shaikh Abdullah got primary education, was shut down in opposition. For twenty years, people could not educate their sons." All ties were completely cut off between Shaikh Saheb and his family after the conversion. His wife Waheed Jahan Begum and daughters longed for visiting Kashmir in the summer holidays and for seeing the elders of the in-law's household, but Shaikh Saheb never consented. Once, Mohsin Abdullah went to the village Kathwa of Jammu and saw his relatives who had converted to Sikhism. A member of this family, Mohan Singh had got education at Aligarh Muslim University and would often come to Abdullah Lodge to see Papa Mian.

One of his contemporary students, Mr. Masood Chaudhary the Vice Chancellor of Baba Ghulam Badshah University of Science and Technology, Rajouri told me that he, too, would accompany Mohan Singh to Abdullah Lodge where he was entertained by Mumtaz Aapa (daughter of Sheikh Abdullah).

Shaikh Saheb published a book on the Prophet's Biography, namely, *Khatimul Anbiya* (Pbuh) in 1953 which reflects his views on Islam. He remained an admirer of both Mirza Ghulam Ahmad Qadyani and Hakeem Nooruddin despite his growing differences with them on religious matters. Shaikh Sb writes, "Irrespective of religious dimensions, if one considers the human aspect of both the great masters, one would find oneself compelled to place both of them on high pedestal among the well-wishers of mankind....It would be injustice to ignore their personal or natural traits on the basis of religious differences....Initially, I was so impressed with the philosophical discourses of (late) Maulvi Nooruddin that I was endeared to the high morals of Islam. Though the three months I was in Mirza Sb's company was accidental, these three months worked well in consolidating and strengthening my religious views." Shaikh also severed his relations with Maulvi Nooruddin who would care for him like his own son and devoted himself to Sir Syed and the Aligarh Movement. In his last moments, Maulvi Sb wished to see Shaikh Abdullah. But he did not go to his house even after his death because he was apprehensive lest Maulavi Saheb should declare him his heir to Qadyanism on his death bed.

Khurshid Mirza, daughter of Shaikh Abdullah, further elaborates on this point, "After the death of Maulavi Nooruddin, Abdullah continued to send money to his widow as long as she lived." She, further says, "I have seen a letter written by Maulvi Sahib's widow to my father, confirming that she received the money that he sent her regularly after Maulvi sahib's death. The letter sounded most affectionate, like it was written by a mother to a long-lost son. Shaikh Abdullah always spoke of Maulvi sahib with deep respect and love and, as a testament to his feelings, a large framed portrait of his mentor still hangs in the main hall of Abdullah Lodge".

Hakeem Nooruddin was among the first to accept the allegiance to Mirza Ghulam Ahmad Qadyani on March 22, 1889. After his death on May, 26, 1908 in Lahore, the Ahmadiya Jamaat appointed Hakeem Nooruddin the first Caliph on May 27, 1908. Thereafter, Mirza Bashiruddin Mahmood Ahmad, son of the founder of the Ahmadiya Jamaat, was appointed the second caliph in 1914 on 14 March.

In 1891, instead of returning to Lahore, Abdullah took the train to Aligarh and joined the Mohammaden Anglo-Oriental College with a letter of introduction and recommendation from Maulvi Noouruddin to Sir Syed. Professor Shamsur Rahman Mohsini writes that Abdullah arrived at Aligarh railway station at midnight, spread out the bedding on the platform and went to sleep. In the morning, when he failed to find a carriage (*tanga*), he asked a coolie to take him to the MAO College. The coolie was as unfamiliar with the town as he was and they both walked to the Scientific Society building, before reaching the Victoria Gate of the university where he ran into an old acquaintance from Lahore, Zafar Ali Khan, who showed him to the college.

He was allotted a room at Kachchi Barrak. In his neighbourhood lived Khwaja Ghulam- us-Saqlain, Khan Bahadur Habibullah, Khan Bahadur Maulvi Nazir Ahmad, retired judge of Kashmir, and the renowned journalist Maulana Zafar Ali Khan. Maulvi Abdul Haq, Maulana Zafar Ali Khan and Dr. Sir Ziauddin Ahmad were some of his hostel fellows. These students belonged to the first generation of Aligarh College and gained fame in various walks of life. They also rendered great services for the country and the community.

Abdullah was admitted to the intermediate level by the Principal, Sir Theodore Morrison. He gave his name as "Abdullah" and his guardian's name as Hakeem Maulvi Nooruddin. Next day he visited Sir Syed and gave him letters from Lahore.

Shaikh Muhammad Abdullah terms his first meeting with Sir Syed as pilgrimage (*ziyarat*). In 1888, when he was fourteen years old and studied in the seventh class, Thakur Das got an opportunity to attend the Mohammadan Education Conference at Lahore. He accompanied his Urdu teacher and Hakeem Nooruddin to hear several Muslim literary scholars. At a meeting, a Lahore editor by the name of Muharram Ali Chishti read out a letter in which Sir Syed was severely criticized. Immediately, the audience was in uproar and decides then and there to boycott the paper. Within a week, the newspaper was closed down.

Thakur Das was deeply affected by this incident and Sir Syed Ahmad's influence played upon his young mind. He lived in Lahore for four years for his matriculation and these four years proved to be a turning point in his life. Thakur Das had read Sir Syed's speeches and publications and had turned into his admirer. Another profound influence on him was that of Maulvi Nooruddin. Thakur Das started studying the life of Muhammad (Pbuh) and the translation of the Holy Quran.

Recollecting his childhood reminiscences, Shaikh Saheb says that Maulvi Nazir Ahmad addressed the gathering in the words, "The quality of today's education is that students do become aware of the goings-on the world over, but their moral education is not satisfactory; the type of education upon which our religious training rests to a considerable extent.

For his FA and BA degrees Shaikh Abdullah opted for English, Philosophy and Persian along with other compulsory papers. Fortunately, he received lessons in English from Mr. Theodore Morison; that of Philosophy from the teacher of Allama Iqbal, Mr. Thomas Walker Arnold; Algebra from Babu Jadav Chandra Chakravarti; Arabic and Persian from Shamsul Ulema Maulana Shibli Nomani and Maulana Abbas Husain and Sanskrit from Pt. Shiv Shanker Tripathi. He took active part in debates and discussions, and various games like Drill, Cricket, Football and

Horse Riding. In 1896 he won the Cambridge Speaking Prize which was awarded to the best debater by the Siddons Union Club." He was influenced by the movement for women's education represented at Aligarh, among other by Khwaja Ghulam-us-Saqlain (his hostel fellow and a close relative of Hali), Prof. Syed Karamat Husain who taught him law. Ghulam-us-Saqlain whose articles regularly appeared in *Aligarh Institute Gazette* and *College Magazine*.

About his student days, Shaikh Abdullah writes in his autobiography, *Mushidat-o-Taassurat*, "Due to all these activities every minor detail of the period is imprinted on the heart." He had become fonder of the college than home.

He took admission to Law course after completing graduation in 1895. Apart from studying law, he also rendered his services as a Librarian at the M.A.O. College. He also rose to become the secretary of the college's Principal, Theodore Beck. Thus, he had won the confidence of Sir Syed and the Principal of the college. He was taking these jobs because he had severed his ties with his family, and was receiving no financial assistance from them.

By 1895, Sir Syed Ahmad's heath deteriorated greatly and he needs young men to help him fight the bigoted mullahs who were trying to hinder his educational mission. A group of Mullahs had issued *fatwas*, or edicts denouncing him as a *kafir*, an apostate and an enemy of Islam, and a British agent. Shaikh Abdullah spent several hours with Sir Syed and by writing articles to newspapers refuted these allegations. Much later, Shaikh Abdullah wrote a pamphlet titled *Kafir aur Kafir gar* in support of Sir Syed's modern methods of education. Here he explained that the so-called mullahs based their verdicts not on the true teaching of Islam, but on the traditions that had emerged after centuries in India that, in their mind, had taken the place of Islam.

Having passed the examination of law, he started practising law in Aligarh as per the instructions from his well-wisher, Sir Syed

Ahmad Khan. He earned much fame in his profession and became one of the respectable figures of Aligarh. For six years, he remained the member of Aligarh Municipal Board as also the President of Aligarh Bar Association. His photograph is still displayed at the office of Aligarh Bar Association. He also enjoyed the membership of U.P. Legislative Assembly. However, these activities did not divest his attention from his chief goal – obtaining the status of Muslim University for the Aligarh College and establishing school for girls.

Shaikh Muhammad Abdullah was married to the younger sister of his close friend, Bashir Mirza on February 2, 1902. Waheed Jahan (1884-1939), his wife was the daughter of Mirza Muhammad Ibraheem Beg whose lineage went to the Mughal rulers. He was a supporter of Sir Syed's campaign for education. That is why, he sent his only son, Bashir Mirza to Aligarh where he came in touch with Shaikh Abdullah, and became his class fellow. Mirza Baig not only imparted his daughter education of Urdu and Persian but also managed European lady tutors for her education. Shaikh Muhammed Abdullah mentions, in one of his writings, the kind of relationship between his friends that was exhibited on the occasion of the marriage. The bridegroom's party arrived in Delhi on 2 February 1902 and stayed at Zeenat Mahal, the property of the Maharaja of Patiala, which was reserved for them by the manager of the estate. Among the notables who attended the wedding ceremony were Nawab Mohsin-ul-Mulk, Sahibzada Aftab Ahmad Khan, Nawab Sir Sultan Ahmad Khan, Khan Bahadur Syed Zainul Abideen, Nawab Sadar-e-Yar-e-Jang Maulvi Habibur Rahman Khan, Syed Zainuddin Khan Bahadur, Syed Abdullah Shah, Ex-political Minister of Maler Kotla, Shamsul Ulama Maulvi Zakaullah, Mr. Ismail Khan — Bar at law, Meer Mahmood Hasan, Meer Faizul Hasan, Haziqul Mulk Hakeem Ajmal Khan, Hakeem Syed Ahmad Khan, Khan Bahadur Maulvi Nazeer Ahmad from the Punjab, Maulavi Shahabuddin advocate, Aligarh, and Khwaja Muhammad Yusuf with both of his sons, Khwaja Muhammad Yahya and Abdul Majeed."

They formed part of Shaikh Abdullah's *barat* and never once let him feel the absence of his own family. A group photograph taken on the occasion has survived the years and tell the story quite well.

After the marriage with an educated Muslim lady, Shaikh Saheb embarked on the mission of solidifying the cause of women's education.

He lived, after marriage, in the locality called Tar Bungalow at AMU Campus for some years. Thereafter, he shifted to a rented house in the Chhatari compound of Nawab Chhatari at Mohalla Rasal Ganj, Aligarh. In 1905, Shaikh Saheb purchased Lala Lalta Prasad Kayasth's Orchard of Nank Rai for Rs. 1,950. The wood in the orchard was sold for Rs. 5,100. He then purchased a pacca plot of 9 bigha in 1910, and raised a mansion there, calling it 'Abdullah Lodge.' He had eight children. His wife, Wahid Jahan, passed away in 1939. About twenty-seven years later, Shaikh also breathed his last in 1965. The graves of both of them are on the right hand side of the Lodge. There are headstones posted on both the graves and the area is fenced. When I reached there to take snaps of the graves, I saw a peacock dancing while the peahen was moving near by. Peacock is the national bird of our country and Shaikh Abdullah's personality and achievement are also of national significance.

One of the important childhood experiences that influenced Shaikh Abdullah's mission and his attitude towards women was that his mother was a victim of domestic violence. Compassionate feelings for his mother proved a boon for women in general in later years. His father Gurmukh Singh was afflicted with polio in his childhood and was, therefore, unable to work hard on the land. The management of the land thus rested with Mohar Singh, his elder brother, whose wife belonged to a wealthy family and was extremely haughty and ill-mannered, especially with Gurmukh Singh's wife who was very beautiful but from a poor family. It pained the child, Thakur Das, to see his mother so humiliated since he loved her very much, and he learnt from an early age about the disrespect faced by those less privileged by wealth and position. Whenever he saw women under pitiable condition, he would become restless. From his student days, he had a lot of compassion for women. There were several incidents in his memory, because of which this feeling had become deep rooted in his heart. While he was studying in Jammu in the lower standard, he heard an old woman (who had served as a slave in the palaces of the kings of Jammu) tell some one that when Raja Sujit Singh, the younger brother of Mahraja Gulab Singh, died twenty-two queens immolated themselves on his funeral pyre; all were very beautiful and most were very young. He also saw the tyranny of a Dogra soldier over a Muslim woman. The woman was in an advance stage of pregnancy. First the soldier forced her to carry loads of firewood on her head.

As a student, Shaikh Abdullah had seen many instances of violence against women. In the neighbourhood of the Lahore Boarding House, lived an old Nawab who had four wives, and would beat them almost everyday.

Upto 1920, students of M.A.O. College had to go to Calcutta (now Kolkata) and Allahabad to take their examinations, because the Aligarh Muslim University had not been operational. Shaikh Saheb also went to Allahabad to appear in the examination of B.A. in 1895, where he came across a sorrowful event. One day he went to the market. He saw that many men and women had gathered, and one stupid fellow was beating a young woman with thorny stick; blood was oozing from her body. From a distance people were asking him not to beat her, but no one tried to go forward and save her. Shaikh Saheb fell in heated arguments with him and even threatened to take legal actions against him.

In a book, named, *Sawanih Umri Abdullah Begum*, Shaikh Saheb mentions another soul-stirring event. He writes, "Once a gentleman told me that in town here was someone who claimed to be the only *Syed*; the rest were hybrids. He had two daughters.

He was not ready to get them married until and unless he could get a pure-blooded *Syed* on both sides (maternal and paternal). At last, when a proposal came from the boy of the second house, he accepted immediately and married off one daughter".

But the members of that second family were even more stupid that the first. The poor girl was trapped. She was not even allowed to visit her father or relatives. Once, while her husband was out, she got the news that her maternal aunt was on her deathbed. She could not restrain herself and took a palanquin to the aunt's house. No sooner had she reached there, than the aunt died.

After a while she realized that she had come without her husband's permission, and if he returned to find that she was not there, he would be outraged. So, she soon returned home. But before her arrival, he had already come back, and was waiting for her in anger. As the lady entered the house, without asking ner anything, the tyrant started beating her with a stick and, continued to do so till she died.

When the foolish father received news of his daughter's death, he came to his son-in law's house, and wept bitterly, making all sorts of allegations; but, finally said that she was lucky to have been killed by him. Both the sadists maintained secrecy and jointly buried the oppressed, murdered girl.

On the fourth day after this incident the foolish man married his second daughter to the same murderer. Apart from producing a deep impact on my heart; this incident drew my attention to the fact that something had to be done so that women did not suffer at the hands of men".

Apart from the above mentioned incidents, there were a number of other incidents that come to his knowledge, and he developed sympathy from women. His law teacher, Maulana Syed Karamat Husain (founder of Karamat Husain Girls College, Lucknow), close friend Khwaja Ghulam-us-Saqlain was in favour of female education. It was also generally believed that Justice

Syed Ammeer Ali, Judge of Calcutta High Court, and Justice Badruddin Tayyabji, Judge of Bombay High Court, also encouraged the idea.

When he was studying law, he wrote an article on the education of Turkish women for Aligarh magazine. By this time he had become quite concerned with the cause of women's education. With the passage of time, his passion grew stronger and he threw himself in the field of women's education. As a student of Aligarh, Shaikh Abudullah was one of the chief exponents of the ideology that echoed towards the end of the 19th century in favour of Muslim women's education. Sir Syed held the view that the campaign for women's education was being launched before the right moment. However, other reformers opined otherwise. In 1884, the proposal of women's education failed to get the majority vote during a discussion among the students of Aligarh Student's Union. But soon, the table was turned, when the students of Aligarh gave thought to getting educated wives. Ghulam-us-Saqlain and Syed Sajjad Haider Yalderam were those who published articles in the 1890s against veil and for the education of Muslim women. Both of them were in the lead of the discussion whereas students supporting the Islamic point of view were delivering speeches against the Western culture.

In one of his articles, named, *Mukalimah*, Shaikh Saheb wrote, "Our religious scholars, be they Hindu or Muslim, they do pay attention towards getting modern education. They do nothing but hurl abusive attributes upon the young minds getting modern education. Muslim *Ulema* never like to talk with them, supposing that the youth getting modern education are damned and cursed by Allah. Therefore, they have nothing to do with religion. On the contrary, the credit of the prosperity and success, visible in the Muslim community today, goes to these very educated youths. They have knowledge; they have craftsmanship and knowledge spread far and wide in the form of translation, etc. due to them. Whatever share Muslims have in government sector, that is because of the knowledge of

English. How come then that we ignore and be careless for this increasing and valuable treasure of tomorrow?

This young generation invites the *Ulema* towards their Islamic duty to be armed with modern education and science and help check the spread of atheism across the country. The *Ulema* say, "It is a matter of grief that many of our youths become atheist under effect of modern education. They don't like even to hear anything about religion." For this, we cannot blame modern education or those getting it. The responsibility, however, lies with those who do not try to check the evil effects, modern education entails.

To check these evil effects from spreading, there is only one solution — knowledge of modern education be made compulsory for those to be appointed for religious education. Efforts should be made to prepare, in great number, such teachers as can solve the problems of the modern educated youths in the light of their own background and understanding. To reap the fruits of modern as well as religious education collectively, it is essential to bridge the gap between the two ideological extremes and only then the two can be of immense profit for each other."

Shaikh Abdullah believed in gender equality and observed that women's empowerment can be achieved through better health and education.

Shaikh Muhammad Abdullah was elected Secretary of the Women's Education section of the All India Muslim Educational Conference in the Session held at Delhi in 1902. He immediately began to work towards creating an atmosphere for the formal education of Muslim women, and decided to test his ideas by sharing them with concerned women.

Since his wife, Waheed Jahan, enthusiastically supported his plan, she invited her educated women friends in Delhi to her parent's house where Shaikh Abdullah put his ideas before them. Many women attended the meeting and endorsed Shaikh Abdullah's ideas. The minutes of the meeting were printed and circulated in various Muslim residential areas. Immediately, the orthodox Muslims were up in arms saying that now western ways are being promoted for women who would be encouraged to attend schools with their faces uncovered!

Despite the initial hostility, Shaikh Abdullah was confident that he was on the right track and that he had a helmate in his wife who could always muster the support of educated women for the cause. He outlined a plan and wanted the subject of women's education to be discussed formally and informally amongst the Muslim classes. He began writing for newspapers and magazines in favour of women's education. 'I was convinced that women needed to be educated to liberate them from social oppression. To educate men and not offer the same facility and exposure to women was like having sunshine in one section of the house and darkness in the other. I firmly believe that when women acquired meaningful knowledge they would be better equipped to protect themselves from exploitation'.

Shaikh wanted to boost self-confidence among women so that they could take the bold initiative on their own and may support them as much as possible. Muslims of that time regarded women's education as the enemy of their so-called culture and civilization and considered the girls' schools to be contrary to the tenets of Islam. The dominating thought was that girls' education would put an end to veil or face-covering. Even women were of this view. They held, "Our simplicity and prestige is due to veil. If it is undone, our prestige will also be done away with." Those who were supporters of women's education were also apprehensive of the consequences. At one place, Shaikh Saheb writes that during the session of the conference held at Amritsar, his kind-hearted teacher Allama Shibli Nomani had asked him in unequivocal terms if veil would be observed in girls' schools or not. Maulana Shibli knew the significance of women's education and wished women to be educated. However, he was an ardent supporter of veil like Sir Syed. Shaikh Sb replied, "Veil will be compulsory as a part of school discipline."

In 1903, *The Aligarh Monthly* published an article by Maulana Abul Kalam Azad (later became the first Education Minister of India), who wrote that the Muslims needed to be aware that their progress was a dependent on the education of their women as it was on the men, because only an educated mother could provide a suitable domestic environment to her children.

To make the condition favourable, Shaikh Saheb took to journalism also. In 1904, he published an Urdu monthly, *Khatoon* and held an exhibition of ladies items on the occasion of the conference. Due to these activities, he had become a popular figure among such women, across the country. With the help of these women, he started promoting the cause of women's education.

After fourteen years of regular publication of *Khatoon*, Shaikh Abdullah published another Urdu monthly, *Raz-e-Taraqqui* in 1946. In the July 1946 issue, he published the results of Muslim Girls' College and High School. They indicate that thirty-six girl's appeared in the High School examination. Of them, thirty girls passed out. Other successful students were: F.A. (Arts) — 23 out of 30; F.A. (Science) — 14 out of 16; B.A. (Arts) — 32 out of 35; B.Sc.— 4 out of 4; M.A. (Final) 5 out of 6; and B.T. — 18 out of 18. All the girls of M.A. (F) were from Geography. The famous novelist, Nigar Salma Rasheed Siddiqui passed the B.A. (Arts) examination with IInd division in 1946. That year, girls excelled the boys.

On looking at the title of the monthly, *Raz-e-Taraqqi,* one may conclude that Shaikh Muhammad Abdullah was the Honorary Secretary of Muslim Girls' College which had not been affiliated to AMU till then.

One may also conclude that the Academic Session of Women's College and Girls' High School started from 1st of September. Admission to B.Sc. was possible only through the entrance test. Conveyance facility was also available for girls residing in the old city.

In the January edition of 1909 of the monthly *Khatoon* the founder of the school, Shaikh Muhammad Abdullah writes under the head of *Zanana Madrasa*, "Presently, about one hundred girls have been enrolled in our Madrasa. Thank God that the progress is satisfactory on all counts. Previously also, we have declared that Indian women have a large share of credit in establishing this Madrasa. First of all, Aliya Begum Sahiba from Bhopal followed by kind-hearted sisters Miss Zohra Faizi Sahiba, Miss Atiya Faizi Sahiba, Mrs. Ali Akbar Sahiba, Sultana Begum Sahiba, etc. paid their valuable attention towards this important task. Her Highness Begum Sahiba Zanjirah and other distinguished ladies extended their wholehearted cooperation towards it. Today, the Madarsa has reached the present status because of the special cooperation of all of them. Allah willing, it will prosper. This sapling will, Allah willing, grow into a huge tree. It will bear fruit and people will get benefit from it. Hopefully, it will be regarded as a beneficial institute and people will come out hand-in-hand to help it grow and bloom. People, who are cooperating with it, will elicit appreciation for their generosity in the days to come....

We also add a note here for the coming generations: "There is an old woman who is ill for a long time. There is a girl child who cannot leave her alone even for a moment. She has to do her household chores. Despite all this, she usually reaches Madrasa at exact nine in the morning. She looks after the services to the lady teachers and remains in Madrasa till five in the evening. She cares least for her child's health, and for her own. She does not even care for her house. All day, she takes care of the girl students thinking that patents have sent them trusting her. Then, she settles disputes of the teachers. In the last, she takes some food."

A fervent promoter of women's education in India, Begum Sultan Jahan, ruler of the princely state of Bhopal granted an aid of Rs. 100 per month for the girls' school. Having received this letter, Shaikh Abdullah made up his mind firmly to establish the school at Aligarh, though his old friend Sahibzada Aftab

Ahmad Khan was against establishing the school at Aligarh but who supported women's education. Shaikh carried the letter with him when he went to Lucknow to take part in the Session of the Conference. He met the Secretary of M.A.O. College, Moulvi Mahdi Ali Khan known as Moshin-ul-Mulk at the late Raja Sir Tasadduq Rasool Khan of Jahangirabad palace. He showed the letter of the Begum of Bhopal to him. Seeing the letter, Nawab Mohsinul Mulk was outraged and expressed his anger in such manner that it still resolve before him, he threw his Turkish cap on the lawn, and said, "People were already opposed to the concept of boys' college and now as they come to know that a girls' school is going to be established at Aligarh, their anger will be multiplied". After a while, when he was cool, Shaikh Abdullah brought the cap and put it on the table before him. Then, he got into a Buggi. Shaikh Sahib also sat in front of him. On the way, Shaikh told him that if he opposed the cause, the coming generations would not pardon him. "Everyone wants that girls should be imparted education. You have opposed it. Then what happened today?" Hearing this, Nawab Saheb smiled and said to him, "Go on with your mission. I have done mine, not yours. It was essential for me to give people the impression that I was no supporter of any school or Madrasa." In this very Session of Lucknow, the resolution regarding the establishment of girls' school in Aligarh was approved.

After this initial success, Shaikh Abdullah had still a lot to do with regard to the collection of funds and making public opinion. In mid-1905, a delegation consisting of students of M.A.O. College and supporters of women's education went to Bombay. They collected a sum of more than Rs. 4000/- The contributors of these donations were wealthy Muslims, particularly, Justice Badruddin Tayyibji and their family. Of those who supported him, were especially Zohra and Atiya Faizi, who helped Shaikh Saheb and Begum Abdullah arranged an exhibition of handicrafts made by women and convened a meeting of Muslim women.

In 1906, after years of discussions in the Muslim Educational Conference, Shaikh Abdullah collaborated with his wife in founding a separate school for girls in Aligarh itself. The School was supported by aristocratic and government subventions, and sufficiently committed to supervision and purdah to win the support of elite. By the time a proper building opened in 1914, the school had a European Principal and English was taught one hour a day: by 1937, it offered degree classes. The School inculcated an ambivalent attitude to western models of female behaviour which were regarded as at once exemplary yet less noble than those sanctioned by Islam at its best. Less ambivalently, it imparted the message of social reform as a characteristic of an aristocratic life, thus fostering a distinctive elite cultural style for women that contrasted with that of the vast majority of the population.

In the following year, the school received a grant of Rs. 1200 from Bhopal. Now, they were determined to choose a place for school. The same year, it was decided to call the Session of the Conference at Aligarh. Shaikh decided to convene a women's meeting in this regard and invited Atiya Faizi, Zohra Faizi, and daughters of Badruddin Tayyibji at Aligarh. It was very hard to organise any women's meeting or exhibition at Aligarh. First, Nawab Mohsinul Mulk agreed and allotted the office of Scientific Society (Hall of Dawakhana Tibbiya College) for the guests, but had to change the venue in the face of strong public criticism. Consequently, the women's meeting was cancelled.

Shaikh Abdullah left early in the morning in search of a house. Throughout the city, no Muslim agreed to let his house be used. However, one of his Parsi friends permitted to use the Shahpurji's building, which is now Dr. Mohan Lal's Eye Hospital. He took the mansion in his possession at once and deployed workers to clean it well. All the guests from Bombay stayed in the mansion. Many samples had been sent from China, Burma, Baghdad, Afghanistan and Kashmir for exhibition. Some samples of embroidery, drawing, handicrafts and calligraphy were sent by

Begum of Bhopal. Queen of Patiala also dispatched specimens of handicrafts. A sum of Rs 250 was sent by Maharaja of Bhavnagar to be distributed as prize. Princess Manohar Kunwar sent a framed painting on velvet. An oil-painting was also put up in the exhibition prepared by the teacher of the princess of Bhavnagar. A large number of women participated in the exhibition. The reason was the over-hyped publicity of the exhibition by the Urdu monthly *Khatoon*.

Proper arrangements of canvass screen were made around the Nizam museum, located in the present S.S. Hall for ladies. Ladies meeting was held in the mansion of Shahpurji which was doubly enclosed by the screens. The meeting in the night of December 29 was women-specific.

In this programme, Shaikh Abdullah brought into light the services and endeavours he had made as the secretary of women's education wing… a large section of Muslim *Ulema* and leaders made violent attacks on Shaikh Abdullah's report. The reason was their failure to establish the Normal School. In the lead of the critics was Syed Mumtaz Ali, who had been removed from the post of the secretary of women's education. Sahibzada Aftab Ahmad Khan said that Mumtaz Ali had changed the topic of discussion. "We have gathered here to listen and analyse the report presented by Shaikh Abdullah. His valuable services for women's education, release of a new magazine, collection of money and organisation of handicrafts for women are some of his achievements which deserve full throat appreciation. We should shun from making him an object of criticism and pulling his leg unjustly."

On December 30, as soon as Shaikh Muhammad Abdullah came out of the Strachey Hall after the programme was concluded, Maulana Shauket Ali gave him a punch on the shoulder from the backside. He was about to attack the second time but the participants intervened and made them reconcile. The incident created a stir among the participants. All the trustees of the

College gathered in front of the mansion of Nawab Sir Fayyaz Ali Khan, i.e., Pahasu House. They decided to demand the cancellation of Shaukat Ali's trusteeship for his rude and uncivilized behaviour. Old Boys of Aligarh also convened a general body meeting at the Strachey Hall to condemn the incident and demanded the cancellation of the trusteeship. They also went to the extant of ousting him from the membership of the Old Boys' Association provided he did not resign from the trusteeship. The news spread far and wide. People started saying about Shaikh, "For the sake of women's education, he does not care even for his life."

As for the Principal of M.A.O. College, Mr. Archbold, he too, considered women's education injurious to the health for M.A.O. College. He opposed the Girls' College to be established at Aligarh near that of Boys' as he regarded it to be the cause of digression and indiscipline among the boys, which will lead to the belief among Muslims that Aligarh College, has been derailed from its initial track. He even threatened that he would resign from the Principalship in opposition to the establishment of girls' school anywhere on the campus of the university. Dr. Sir Ziauddin was also of the same opinion. He said in very clear terms that girls' school should be opened at the other extreme of the city if it is to be done at all, so that it may not affect the Boys' College. Honorary Secretary of the college, Viqarul Mulk met Shaikh Abdullah to know the details of the incident. Shaikh Saheb replied: "The College staffs live with family on the campus or in nearby areas, and nobody thinks of it. So, if a Girls' College is established far from the Boy's College and which is safe by high walls, it will not make any difference." As a result, Viqarul Mulk was convinced by Shaikh Abdullah.

He filed a petition to the Lt. Governor of Utter Pradesh in 1906. In the petition he said: "Muslims are extremely ignorant towards girls' education. There is not a single girls' school throughout the length and breadth of the country. We want to establish a girls' school at Aligarh which is possible only with the government's support. Therefore, kindly grant a delegation of Muslims to submit a memorandum in this regard. The office of the Governor enquired of the names of the delegates. And so, all the leaders of the community agreed to enrol themselves in the delegation. Those who consented to meet the Governor included Nawab Mohsinul Mulk, Nawab Sir Fayyaz Ali Khan, Nawab Muzammilullah Khan, Nawab Raja Tasadduq Rasul of Jahangirabad, Maharaja Sir Ali Muhammad Khan of Mahamoodabad, Sahibzadah Aftab Ahmad Khan, Raja Naushad Ali Khan from Jahangirabad, Maulvi Muhammad Waseem Advocate from Lucknow and Khwaja Ghulam- us-Saqlain Advocate from Meerut.

The Governor Sir James Latouche fixed the date of August 6, 1906 for appointment. But, most of the delegates refused to go on one or the other excuse. The only persons who went to the Governor House were Raja Naushad Ali, Khwaja Ghulam-us-Saqlain and Maulvi Muhammad Waseem. The first question that the Lt. Governor asked to why the other great personalities mentioned had not come. Shaikh Abdullah replied, "That the reason for that was very clear because till then the government had not paid any attention to the education of Muslim women, so the Muslim landlords and wealthy people, not only neglected it, but considered it an irrelevant thing. The same thing had happened to MAO College Aligarh as till then the government had not helped, so the general Muslim population also did not care. The Governor said that the government would provide financial support if any Madrasa is established. He then asked to Abdullah to go ahead and open the school and then report to him, after which they would send an inspector, and if her report was favourable then only would government get the grant.

Therefore, Shaikh Sahib left for the search of a Muslim woman teacher along with the friends Maulvi Ehtishamuddin and Azmat Ali. Unfortunately, they could not find even a single lady teacher in whole of Lucknow who might teach women at Aligarh.

Somebody told about Dr. Ruqayya Begum. On searching for her they found a musical drum (dholak) hanging in the verandah. Besides Lucknow, search for a lady teacher was also on in Aligarh. Finally, they took Mrs. Abdullah from Delhi, but there, too, they failed to find a lady for the purpose of teaching in Aligarh.

After a wild goose chase, they came to know about a teacher who was able to teach Holy Quran and who also knew Urdu. But she was unable to leave Delhi. They found her house at last. But she declined the offer outright. After much persuasion, she agreed on the condition that her family members would also accompany her and live with her. There were three members in the family besides her husband; her mother and daughter. Shaikh Abdullah accepted her all the conditions. She came to Aligarh along with her family. Her name was Akhtari Begum. At Aligarh, Shaikh Abdullah rented a house at Rs. 2 per month far from the College campus, at Tantan Para, Upperrkot region, in which the Akhtari and her family began living. Thus, the girls' school came into existence far from the city just like a hospital, meant for the untouchable. Girls from the nearby areas began going there and learning Holy Quran. But, the formal inauguration of the school was made in 1907. As for the conveyance of the girls, three sedans or palanquins were arranged, carried by six employees under the care of Akhtari's husband. A scholarship was sanctioned for her daughter and her mother was employed for cleaning and washing the wooden tablets to practise writing on wooden slates. In a way, the entire family of the teacher was engaged in school's business. Waheed Jahan Begum and both her sisters, i.e., Sikander Jahan Begum and Saeed Jahan Begum would visit the school daily at Tantan Para to teach and train the girls entrusting their children to servants at Chhatari Compound. These teachers regarded the girls as their own daughters. Whenever they came to know that there were some poor girls who could not bring their lunch, they would invite them to their own lunch, and mostly skipped their lunch.

The Lt. Governor was informed about this school. A lady Inspector of Schools Miss Ganja inspected it and just after one and a half month from the submission of the report, the school administration began receiving a sum of Rs. 250 (Two hundred and fifty) per month. Besides, the government also granted a sum of Rs. 17,000 (Seventeen Thousand) in one go. The number of sedans was increased with the increase of students and one portion of the house was converted into a Boarding House. Akhteri's mother was appointed its warden. With the growing popularity of the school, eve-teasers also began appearing. They would lift the curtains of the sedans and eve-tease the students. Shaikh Muhammad Abdullah ambushed and caught some of them. He began beating them with a stick. Thereafter, none dared pass by the sedans. The building which housed the earliest school is still in the same form and condition. Bilquees Aapa ran another school, named; *Sirajul Uloom Niswan College* for a long time after Shaikh Saheb had left this building. It was divided into two, after she left for Pakistan. The main part is Saeed Manzil, whereas the second part was purchased by Police Inspector Riyaz Muhammad Khan. He had two sons: Fayyaz Rifat and Ashfaq Muhammad Khan. While the former had been the Director of Lucknow Door Darshan, the latter was the Bureau Chief of the Press Trust of India (PTI). I used to visit the house every week. All the three daughters of the Inspector also got education in the Girls' High School and Women's College. The eldest one, Mukhtar Aapa is a teacher in a Govt. School.

In 1910, the school was shifted to a rented house at Bani Israilan for lack of sufficient space. Later on, the school was shifted to its main building situated at Marris Road. When Shaikh Saheb vacated this building also, the Municipal Board ran a school, namely, School No: 16 for a long period. Now, this building has reached its original owner. One of the retired employees of A.M.U., Habeeb Israili has transformed it into a Marriage Hall, named, Ar-Reehan.

On November 7, 1911, the Lt. Governor of U.P. Mr. Porter's wife laid the foundation stone of the first Girls' School. This was the first function to be organized on such a grand scale and it was then that people learnt that a hostel was being constructed for girls outside the city, and construction work had already started. The building used to be a part of the Hall of Waheedia Hostel, where the stone inscription exists even today. First of all, the founder of the school constructed the Boarding House so that the girls coming from far off places could get place to stay in. This decision was criticised, too. Some of the critics said ironically: "Instead of purchasing horse first, you've taken its whip. Traditionally, school is constructed first and then hostel. But you're going against the tradition." On February 14, 1914, the ruler of Bhopal, Sultan Jahan Begum inaugurated the Waheedia Hostel. On the day first, nine girls were admitted to it. Special arrangements were made for veil; so the walls were raised on the pattern of a prison. No man was allowed to enter the Hostel, except the sweeper and the bearer of water-skin. Some parents even raised their voice against these two men. Two parents even withdrew their daughters from the hostel. On the occasion of the inauguration of this first hostel, the ladies who came from across the countries included Faizi sisters from Bombay, sister of Maulana Abul Kalam Azad — Aabru Begum, wife and daughter of Sir Mian Muhammad Shafi from Lahore, mother of the Pakistan's Prime Minister Zulfiqar Ali Bhutto, Begum Shahnawaz Bhutto and other respectable ladies from the Punjab and Hyderabad apart from Aligarh. Maulvi Mahboob Alam, editor *Paisa* and Maulvi Syed Mumtaz Ali of monthly Tehzeeb-un-Niswan, Lahore also grace the function.

In her inaugural address, Begum Bhopal made an indication towards the tightening of the doors of the Hostel. She regarded it as continuing obstacles in the path of girls' education.

Farha Nizami, an alumna writes about this concern, "When Begum Sahiba tried to enter the Hostel, she did unlock the door but could not open it, which was newly fitted. After many efforts, Begum Abdul Majeed Khwaja succeeded to open it but she hurt herself. On this incident, Begum Zanjeera said, 'Ladies, see these are the doors to women's education, and we are successful in opening them, though it took meticulous efforts and hardship."

In the beginning, nine girls were admitted in the hostel. Among those three were Shaikh Abdullah's daughter, three were the daughters of Abdullah Begum's second sister, one was Abdullah begum's friend Maimoona Begum's daughter and two others were from Bulland Shahr.

Waheed Jahan Begum began to reside in the hostel and left her two children at home in the care of maid-servants. In those days, there was no population around the hostel, and, during the night, people were afraid to move around even within the campus. Though there were watchmen and dogs all the time, yet little girls could not be left on their own, so Abdullah Begum and some teachers stayed with them. When people learnt that Abdullah Begum herself lived in the hostel, they took a sign of relief. Many parents were very happy by this move, and the number of girls began increasing. Meer Vilayat Husain himself admitted his daughters to the Hostel who completed their education from this school and passed the medical examination from Lady Harding, Delhi.

In the initial days, mothers of girls had also been allowed to stay with their daughters for their satisfaction. These mothers watched Begum Abdullah's motherly treatment towards these girls and handed over their girls happily to Begum Abdullah and said, "O Bibi, we've left the girls with you in faith. Now, the prestige of our family rests with you." It was a great sacrifice on the part of Begum Abdullah to live in one of the rooms of the Hostel away from her family. Shaikh Saheb writes, "Throughout India, this was the only hostel for Muslim girls."

With the increase of girl students, levels of education were also raised. As long as the Madarsa was in the city, the level was upto Primary. After the construction of hostel, the school progressed beyond the level of Primary. In the academic session 1916-17, three girls appeared in the examination of Anglo-Vernacular Middle class, and all passed with distinction. Girls began garnering interest in education and wishing to pass the Matric, too, for which qualified lady teachers were required. Until that period, no fee was charged for tuition or food or lodging. And Begum Abdullah would receive money every month from her husband. Later on, Nizam of Hyderabad, Nawab of Tonk, Nawab of Bhawalpur and Nawab of Bhopal began granting generous aids. Even the U.P. Government also increased the annual grant from three thousand to seven to eight thousand rupees. Graduate and post graduate lady teachers could be appointed. Thus, the girls of that school began appearing in the examinations of middle and matric.

In 1921, the school was granted the status of High School by the U.P. Government. Some girls appeared in the examination of U.P. Board. All of them passed. Due to excellent results, some of them were also granted scholarships. In July 1922, three girls passed the High School examination. Of them, two were none, but the daughters of Shaikh Abdullah himself while the third was that of a judge, Khan Bahadur Muhammad Husain. On May 22, 1951, Shaikh Abdullah transferred his non-movable property to the name of Women's College and Girls' High School.

Shaikh Abdullah's wife, Begum Waheed Jahan would reach the school daily in the morning. She looked after the management and took care of the girls. Had she been born to a Christian family, she must have been awarded the Nobel Prize like Mother Teresa. All her life was dedicated to the service of mankind. That was a period when epidemic plague broke out. On getting suspicious, girls began avoiding the affected students. On the contrary, Begam Abdullah would remain close to them throughout night. She pleaded, "If ever I caught the infection, I will die but once. But the girl, at least, would feel that she was not without mother." Referring to this incident in a meeting of the Executive Council, Shaikh Saheb once said, "How selfless women are! If any boy was hit by plague in our university, no teacher or professor might have taken him in his lap the night over."

Given the condition of veil in that period, Shaikh Abdullah and Mrs. Abdullah were very conscious about it. There were arrangements of horsecarts and buses for girls coming from the city. Once, the bus broke down on the way. So, she herself went to the girls' homes to bring them. All the letters addressed to the hostel-girls were first handed over to her and she gave them to girls after tallying the handwriting with that of their parents. Once, she checked her own daughter, Khursheed Mirza's letter. Khursheed Mirza has given a very interesting account of this event.

The Education Minister of Uttar Pradesh, Mr. Sampurnananda, who was much hated among Muslims for his anti-Urdu policies, visited the college in 1938 and inspected the Boarding House. After inspection, he said, "I was doubtful about the management behind the veil, but our surprised to find how beautifully and disciplined people can live even after observing veil." Not only that, he also granted a sum of twenty thousand rupees for building construction and sanctioned a grant of two thousand rupees annually for the Boarding House.

Shaikh Muhammed Abdullah writes: "I have never seen a rich man granting huge sums of money on the daily needs or education except Nawab Sir Fayyaz Ali Khan and Nawab Sir Muzammilullah Khan....Our rich brothers are prejudiced against girls' education. Therefore, spending money on women's education is considered to be a sin or an act near that. For some time now, they have started sending their girls to Aligarh school for education, though they must be taking that to be an act of sin. But if it comes to spending money on school, they are sure to regard it as a grave sin."

During the period of Sir William Marris's Governorship, it was decided to start an Intermediate College. He had been collector at Aligarh, too. He was well aware of the charming personality and valuable achievement of Shaikh Muhammad Abdullah. He helped a lot in starting Intermediate classes. He also doubled the grant and gave more than fifty thousand rupees for the construction of new hostel. Sultania Hostel is one of them. Thus, two hostels had been erected in Shaikh Sahib's life. In 1926, girls started appearing for the Intermediate examination and in 1929; U.P. Board granted the school the status of Intermediate College. Shaikh Muhammad Abdullah wanted to affiliate the college to the Aligarh Muslim University. So, in 1939, the affiliation was obtained. Taking into consideration the growing number of girls, it was decided to start B.A. classes, as well.

In 1935, the Session of Muslim Education Conference was convened at Rampur under the presidentship of Syed Husain Bilgarami. Shaikh Abdullah also participated in the meeting and offered the plan of a Girls' Degree College at Aligarh. Many participants favoured the proposal. While criticizing the opponents of girls' education, Shaikh Abdullah wrote many articles. When Sir Shah Muhammad Sulaiman was appointed the new Vice Chancellor, he gave his consent for the establishment of Women's College on the request of Shaikh Abdullah. Simultaneously, the University Administration also sanctioned a grant of five thousand rupees annually in 1937-38. B.A. classes also began to be held. Thereafter, the university allowed girls to take admission in P.G. Classes.

Boarding arrangements for the students of P.G. Classes were made in the same hostel. A Bill of amendment in the university-laws was tabled in the Parliamentary winter Session in November with regard to the establishment of the Women's College. The Bill was fervently supported by Sir Muhammad Yaqoob and Mr. P. N. Sapru, whereas Pt. Hirday Nath Kanzru proposed that girls should be given opportunities or rights to education equal to those of boys in the Muslim University. Thus, he opposed the independent establishment of girls' college. This Bill was passed without much discussion.

The grant of five thousand rupees given by the university to the college was insufficient. Shaikh Abdullah did away with the affiliation of the college to the university. He sought the help of his classmate, Dr. Sir Ziauddin, the then M.L.A. approached the U.P. Government once again. In this way, this Women's College of the University was included for the aid of UP Government. In 1944, the U.P. Government granted a sum of eighteen thousand and five hundred rupees. And the Managing Committee of the Women's College kept on shouldering the responsibilities of the college up until the partition of the country.

Up to 1944, girls studying in B.T., M.A., and other P.G. Courses used to stay at Girls' Hostel but its doors were shut for the students of Women's College after the college came under the support of U.P. Govt. in 1944. Now, their classes began to be held in the university and therefore, arrangements were made for separate screens in the classrooms of the university for girls.

The first Education Minister of India after independence, Maulana Abul Kalam Azad visited Aligah Muslim University on February 20, 1949, when Dr. Zakir Husain was the Vice Chancellor, to deliver the convocation address. On that occasion, Shaikh Muhammed Abdullah also invited him to Women's College and informed him of the financial problems of the college. Maulana Azad sanctioned a grant of nine lakh rupees annually inview of the excellent performance of the college and promised to include it into the University Budget. He kept his word. Thus, the ties of the college with the Government of Uttar Pradesh became a part of the Aligarh Muslim University itself. This institution has been making progress since 1949, in terms of new construction and new courses of study.

Paying tribute to the services of Shaikh Abdullah, Prof. Aal-e-Ahmad Suroor, who was a distinguished Urdu critic and an awardee of Padma Bhushan, says, "Sir Syed regarded boys' education more important. He was of the view that girls would automatically get education if the boys are educated. Shaikh Abdullah made girls' education goal of his life. He laid the foundation of a school in the face of harsh criticism and hill moving resistance. The school was transformed first into an

Intermediate and then a Degree College with the passage of time. His wife, known as Aala Bi was his right hand in the mission. The kind of national passion and enthusiasm to help and serve the community, which was common among the educated youths in Sir Syed's time, was found in its consummation in the heart of Shaikh Abdullah, too. He also rendered his valuable services for the sustenance and development of Urdu, language. Whenever he met with people, he used to talk of the condition of Muslims in India."

A Professor in the Department of Surgery, Jawaharlal Nehru Medical College at Aligarh Muslim University and the author of *Jawab-e-Dost*, Dr. Neseem Ansari pays his tributes to Shaikh Abdullah for his magnificent services in these words, "Among Sir Syed's students, there emerged a mad lover, named Shaikh Abdullah. In those days, ignorant people did not educate their girls lest the girls should know writing letters on being mature. Shaikh Abdullah washed clear their minds. In that context, think over the-then situation prevailing everywhere and see today's college. Then, the girls would go to school in the sedans all covered. Despite this, if a bit of their veil was visible people would make hue and cry. How patiently Shaikh Abdullah welcomed every kind of criticism! However, he never let his will swerve even for a while. Today, products of this college include lawyers, doctors, surgeons, engineers, university professors and ministers in the Government. All this could be possible because of his iron-will and unshakable belief in the Almighty, God. He would say, 'Man is superior to all the creatures because of his will to change the direction of winds and has the power to transform pessimism into optimism."

Shaikh Muhammad Abdullah received many awards and honours for his diverse services in the field of women's education. In 1904, he was appointed as the Trustee of M.A.O. College. He was also the member of the Executive Council and the university court, the supreme governing body of the university. In 1931, he also enjoyed the post of the Honorary Treasurer. In recognition to his public services, he was awarded the title of *Khan Bahadur* in 1935. In 1950, Aligarh Muslim University awarded him the honorary doctorate of Law. After independence, the Indian Government gave him the prestigious civilian award *Padma Bhushan* in 1964.

His family was regarded as progressive and broad-minded in Aligarh. His eldest daughter was born on August 25, 1905. Her name was Rasheed Jahan (1905-1952). She was the eldest of all seven brothers and sisters. In 1929, she obtained the Degree of M.B.B.S. from Delhi's Lady Hardings College and joined the government service. When she was working in Lucknow, around 1931-32, she met Mahmooduz Zafar, Ahmad Ali, Sajjad Zaheer. They were socialist and wrote fiction to express the injustices in society especially towards women. She was attracted to the new wave of poets Majaz, Ali Sardar Jafri, Kaifi Azmi, Faiz and others. On October 14, 1932, she married Mahmooduz Zafar, an Oxford graduate. Her house became a rendezvous for leftist intellectual; writers and political workers. Rasheed Jahan was better known as a Progressive writer, and with her coterie of friends wrote against social conventions and false interpretation of religion.

However the anthology that published in 1932 called *Angare* created a furore and was banned. She was referred to as "Rasheed Jahan Angare wali". However, later under the influence of Prem Chand, she was perhaps the first woman writer in Urdu to address herself squarely, consistently and forcefully to the myriad problems putting to plight of women in Indian society, "she can rightly be called Urdu literature's 'first angry young woman", writes Hamida Saaiduzzafar in her autobiography. She died of cancer on July 29, 1952 at the age of 47 in Moscow while undergoing medical treatment there. She was buried there. Many books have been written on her in Hindi, Urdu and English.

Shaikh Abdullah's second daughter, named Khatoon Jahan, was also a highly educated lady. After doing her B.A. in India, she went to Leeds University, England to do her M.A. On her return, she became the Principal, Women's College, Aligarh, for some years; she then went to Calcutta ,and became the Principal of the Muslim College. She was married to a resident of Aasansol, Mian Abu Muhammad Lais Qamrain who was also educated in London and worked in the Reserve Bank of India.

The third daughter Mumtaz Jahan did her M.A. form Lucknow University and Diploma in Teaching from the University of Bristol, England. She was married to Col. Haider Khan, Professor of chemistry. She rendered her services as the Principal of Women's College for thirty years. She was a ready help for every one, and was also strict at discipline. Her daughter, Shahla Haider, was the Director of the D.A.V.P. in the Ministry of Information and Broadcasting, Govt. of India. The younger brother of Miss Shahla Haider, viz, Salman Haider has been Ambassador of India in various countries of the world. Also, he has served as the Secretary to the Ministry of Foreign Affairs, Government of India.

Shaikh Abdullah's son, Mohsin Abdullah, graduated from the Aligarh University in Physics in 1930 and he obtained the Degree of LL.B. During his study period, Mohsin was also elected a cabinet member of the Student's Union. He left his legal practice and joined the Film industry in Bombay. Shaikh Abdullah did not like the decision of his son. He says, "We are not on good terms because of leaving the practice of law. This is due to irregular work, insufficient income and no social status. The wife of Mohsin Abdullah, viz. Shahida, also worked in the film industry and came to be known as a successful heroine of her times. She was known as 'Naina'. They bore a son, viz., Tariq Abdullah, presently in Canada. He is the actual heir to the family. Shahida divorced her husband and married the film producer, Mr. W. Z. Ahmad. Mohsin Abdullah also married another girl from film-city. Unfortunately, she also left him and settled in Pakistan. Mohsin Abdullah passed his last period of life in Abdullah Lodge and died there. I was present at the funeral processions of Mumtaz Aapa and Mohsin Abdullah. Shaikh Abdullah also wrote many books and booklets on the religious teachings and moral values apart from his services to women's education. A devout Muslim, he founded the Aligarh Society for propagation of Islam in 1908. When the dead body of Mohsin was ready for funeral prayer, no Maulvi agreed on leading the same because none had ever seen him offering Prayer. Munshi Shahid Husain Khan came forward and provided for his funeral and the related expenses of the deceased. It is a matter of grief that son of a great legend met such a sorry end. Few heads carried his body to the graveyard.

The fifth child of Shaikh Abdullah was very bright. She was Khurshid Jahan (1918-1989). Born on March 4, 1918, she was married to Akbar Mirza after having passed the examination of High School. Though educated parents were not ready to marry her at such a tender age, but Dr. Rashid Jahan created a favourable atmosphere at house and she was married at the age of 15 years. From the early age, she was fond of singing, music and dancing. Her husband, Akber Mirza was a Police Officer. Dancing and singing in Officers' Club had become a part of her daily routine, which led her entry into Film Industry. She worked in many Indian films by the name of Renuka Devi. Later on, she worked in many hit Pakistani TV serials, such as *Kiran Kahani, Zer Zabar Pesh, Parchoon Wala, Shama, Parchain, Aagahi and Afshan*. She became one of the Pakistan's best-known television characters and was honoured with the President Medal by General Zia ul Haq in 1985. She died on 8th February 1989. Her daughter, Lubna Kazim, got a book published in English, based on the memories of Khursheed Mirza in 2005, namely, *A Woman of Substance*, from India.

Birjees Jahan is the youngest daughter of Shaikh Saheb. She was married to an ICS officer, Ahmad Nazeer Qidwai. He had also been the chief secretary of Assam. His son Rasheed Khalid Qidwai married Nina Lal who is the Chief Executive Officer of Hong Kong-Shanghai Banking Corporation (HSBC) and is the highest paid Indian woman. Of all the children of Shaikh Saheb, only Birjees Aapa is alive and is presently the Trustee of Abdullah Lodge. She always attends programmes of Women's College and is based in Delhi, and is constantly in touch with Aligarh.

Today the premises of the Abdullah Lodge are in use for the Abdullah Nursery and Primary School. The Vice Chancellor of Jamia Millia Islamia and the well-known historian, Prof. Mushirul Hasan told me that he had been a student of Abdullah Nursery. My son, Talha Israr, and daughter, Subia Rahat, have also got education up to class V in the said school. My daughter has done engineering in Architecture and works in a reputed construction company in Delhi. The Students' Union of Women's College also runs a school for poor children in the same building, named, Papa Mian School. Some Lady teachers also help the school administration financially.

Shaikh Muhammad Abdullah also established a female education association in 1904 in order to disseminate his mission of women's education. Ladies' conferences were also held in different parts of the country under the banner of the association. Shaikh Saheb remained its secretary till death. Thereafter, Prof. Hamida Saeeduz Zafar, Institute of Ophthalmology was appointed secretary. She was succeeded by Alhaj Obaidur Rahman Khan Sherwani and for the last eight years, the former Principal of Women's College, Prof. Zakiya Athar Siddiqui has been rendering her services as its secretary. She has also the credit of convening many conferences on women's education with mutual cooperation of Duty Society and All India Muslim Educational Conference. Women's study centre is also the fruition of meticulous efforts made by Female Education Association.

The old students of Women's College also established A.M.U. Old Girls, Association. The Association publishes a magazine. Its office is at Hamid Manzil. Besides, there is also a Ladies Club under the stewardship of the wife of the Vice Chancellor. In this way, educated women have sustained the candle lit by Shaikh Abdullah. Ladies Club also established a literacy centre known as Ismat literacy centre after the name of Ismat Chughtai, an illustrious daughter of this institution.

romantic. Fear, enshrined in the hearts of girls, and a few romance was attached to this name. In those days, even black, lean and weak boys also appeared healthy from far. On seeing them from near, girls were disheartened. Majority of the boys were black, lean and unattractive.

Now, boys go the college independently in the functions and on the occasions of sale, girls play host to them. They are no more *Koriale*, but good looking and handsome.

Old girls who are now professors, lecturers, and teachers say with a sigh of sorrow, "Boys, in our times, were handsome. Now, it is rubbish."

In fact, the veil, which separated them, had many a dream, which is ruined. Now, girls don't get disturbed or nervous to see boys, rather, consider them students of their own category. It does not mean that romance disappeared with veil. Now, there must be enormous affairs taking place and marriages having been solemnised.

There are certain benefits, no doubt. When the veil is removed, some cheap and ignoble emotions which are born just on the basis of imagination and lead to some great mental uneasiness, are tranquilled and comfort each other. Reality comes to the fore. It becomes easy to understand each other as a human being, and not only as a person of opposite sex. Possibility of affairs with unknown persons becomes less and life gets attractive and enjoyful on the basis of firm relations.

There were no provisions for B.A. in Aligarh after F.A. My bank account still had sufficient money. The father allowed me to take admission in the I.T. College of Lucknow....Two years which I spent in Lucknow proved of great importance in my life. The vision got broadened. New windows were opened."

Aligarh Muslim University always attached great importance not only to women's education but also to women's esteem. Appointing a woman the first Chancellor of a Muslim University was a very radical step. In a society of Muslims where religious decrees (*Fatwe*) were issued against women's education, people of Aligarh always remained firm on their stand and promoted their broad-mindedness. In 1920, Sultan Jahan Begum was appointed the first Chancellor of the University. Begum Sahiba was a fervent supporter of women's education. During her tenure as the Chancellor, she spoke on the importance of women's education in her first convocation address in 1922. She said" "We must not neglect the question of female education which unhappy has been long neglected in the past. Now, that you have a University of your own and the power to prepare syllabi fully able to meet your demands and to adopt the courses and examinations to your needs, a moment's today is unpardonable. You already possess a good girls' school here which can easily be converted into a university institution. But its foundation must be laid not on the basis of foreign curricula, but on one broad principle of our ancient culture and national tradition.

The distinction between the education of men and women is fundamental; each should in its sphere, be adequate to meet its peculiar requirements. The scheme of female education should especially be framed to meet the requirements of the sphere in which women are called upon to play their role of life and in every aspect the teachings of Islam must find a conspicuous place in it."

Delivering the third annual convocation address on January 26, 1925, Chancellor, Sultan Jahan Begum of Bhopal was happy to see the name of a Muslim girl in the list of successful candidate in B.A. She said that the Prophet has spoken much for the education of girls and there is no reason why the parents hesitate to send their daughters to school. For a civilized society, the education of both the boys and girls is essential".

The girls' school established by Shaikh Abdullah and Aala Bi had become High School when the Aligarh Muslim University started women's education. Just after three years from the establishment of the university, Pasha Begum got the Degree of Graduation in 1924 and thus she had the honour of being the first woman graduate of the AMU. In 1926, Amtul Rasheed Begum and in 1928, Puttan Khairun Nisa Goshal got the Bachelor's degree with second division. As for post graduate education, Miss R. Sarojini Devi was the first M.A. in English in 1931. Mrs. G.M. Khan was the first woman who got the degree of B.T. in 1927.

Aligarh Muslim University had also set up Board of Council for the development and promotion of women's education. Girls were allowed to take admission in any course. The Vice Chancellor was the President of the Board of Women's Education while the other members included Pro Vice-Chancellor, two members of the Executive Council and three members of the Academic Council. The Registrar was the ex-officio secretary of the Board. The task of the Board was to make arrangements for screens in the classrooms and the examination rooms for girls. Unlike boys, girls were not bound to attend the classes, and attendance was not compulsory for them. In 1932, Khan Bahadur Shaikh Abdullah and Khan Bahadur Syed Zainuddin were appointed as the members of the Executive Council. As for the Academic Councils, M. M. Sharif, educationist Khwaja Ghulam-us-Syedain and renowned historian Prof. Muhammad Habib were its members.

In the functions of convocation, women were not allowed to come on stage to receive degrees from the Chief Guest. Their degrees were dispatched to them on their residential addresses. At the Annual Convocation in 1939 a batch of Girls candidates was, for the first time in the history of the institution, conducted to the dias by their lady Provost to receive their degrees.

The distinguished Urdu novelist and writer, Qurratul Ain Haider, the daughter of the first Registrar of the University, Sajjad Haider Yalderem sheds some more light on this issue, "In the period when the (Late) father was the Registrar of the University, some *Ulema* objected even to women's presence from behind the screens on the occasions of convocation. In response, Amma's article was published in which she wrote that even fish breathe in the open air after every few seconds and raise their head out of water. You don't approve of even this much for us. In 1920, when Kamal Ata Turk banned veil legally, the father who was already a great lover of Turkish life asked Amma to abandon it."

In 1920, at the time of the establishment of the Aligarh Muslim University, first generation trained and taught by Sir Syed had practically stepped in real life. Most of them had begun participating in the freedom struggle and some students of M.A.O. College had also joined the university staff. Meanwhile, Mahatama Gandhi's Swadeshi *Aandolan* and condemnation of English education had taken place. As a result, some of the enthusiastic students of the university announced the establishment of a new university by the name of Jamia Millia Islamia.

The first generation of M.A.O. College began educating their girls and there came a revolutionary change in the upcoming generation. The daughters of Shaikh Abdullah, Meer Vilayat Husain and Dr. Sir Ziauddin studied in the school. The elder daughter of Ziauddin, Ijaz Fatima; and Meer Vilayat Husain's daughter Zubaida Shaikh — all of them got the Degree of medicine from the Lady Hardings Medical College, Delhi. Dr. Ijaz Fatima established a hospital in Karachi, Pakistan after her deceased father's name, and later on, established Dr. Zainuddin Medical University. In the history of Aligarh, she is the first to establish a Medical University with her husband.

In the second decade of the 20th century, the Romantic Movement also got considerable contribution of Aligarh. At that time, romantic poetry of Hasrat Mohani was very popular. In the 1930s, Aligarh Muslim University had become the centre of the modern thinking and cultural influence on the new generations of Muslims. The Progressive Movement provided a new turn to the Urdu literature. In this venture also, Aligarh did not lag behind. Akhter Raipuri, Sibt-e-Hasan, Khwaja Ahmad Abbas, Hayatullah Ansari, Saadat Hasan Manto, Majaz, Jan Nisar Akhtar, Ali Sardar Jafri, Moin Ahsan Jazbi and Aal-e-Ahmad Suroor. All were the students of Aligarh. Founder of the Communist Party, Dr. K.M. Ashraf and Dr. Abdul Aleem were among teachers. Dr. Kunwar Muhammad Ashraf had also been the president of student's Union in 1925. When the branch of Progressive Writers'

Association was opened at Aligarh, Aal-e-Ahmad Suroor was appointed as its secretary. In the meetings of the progressive writers, more women participated than men.

This communist atmosphere of Aligarh cannot be described by any one better than the wife of Akhtar Raipuri. She says, "Mahmooduz Zafar, Dr. Rasheed Jahan, Akhtar Raipuri, Sibt-e-Hasan, K.M. Ashraf, Ather Ali and Majaz would hold meetings in Neeli Chhatri. Communism was getting hold in the University in that time and we all wanted it to be strengthened and widespread as soon as possible. All efforts were being made to free the country. You, the ladies, should also participate in it. On the day after tomorrow, I and Sibt-e-Hasan are going to Delhi to bring Jawaharlal Nehru to Aligarh. Prof. Habib Saheb would be the host. You all keep going there. So, go there with Jamila. Maybe you awake after listening to him. If half of the population remains passive, how can the goal be achieved? No doubt, we did understand these things and we found a little enthusiasm taking place in the hearts. Akhtar handed over to me the magazine, namely, *Saqui*. His short story, *Andha Bhikari* had been published in it.

Through Safia, we knew that Akhtar Husain Raipuri had created a stir in the university. A weekly newspaper, somewhat communist and written in hand was pasted on the wall of the hostel. Soon, its copies were pasted on the walls of every hostel. All its contents would be pro-communism, based on encouragement for freedom struggle, Hindu-Muslim unity and opposition of the English. It was compulsory for the Muslim students to come for morning prayers (Fajr). Akhter would go for prayer clad in Arabic cloth and a rosary of one thousand beeds in the hand. The poor Khairi was helpless and cold take no action against him even as the boys laughed to see him in that attire.

Hamida Umar, daughter of the well-known Urdu novelist Zafar Umar, became a fan of Akhtar Raipuri's short stories. In that period, Safia had fallen in love with Jan Nisar Akhtar.

After my acceptance, Akhter wrote a letter to my father, "A humble soul, who is alone but is in further wild chase of knowledge in spite of the wealth of knowledge in his bosom, implores you, for the hand of your daughter Hamida Umar. If granted, I'll be highly obliged, if not, I'll have no grudge against you but against Allah who is Most Merciful, Most Compassionate."

The mother said to me..."Listen then, your father has decided to marry you with Akhtar Husain. I opposed to the best of my authority, but in vain. Now, I think the only solution is that you write on a piece of paper, "I do not agree with your decision." Then he will be helpless. Abruptly, I asked her, "But why?" She replied," O.K. then listen! The boy is a writer. I think every poet, writer and painter expects his wife to see life with his own glasses, which is impossible as every one has one's own view. Ups and downs are with all, but to put up with such people is the toughest job in the world. Furthermore, a gentle girl like you can never do that. Therefore, this match will not prove to be successful." On December 30, 1935, both were married. Maulvi Abdul Haq (Baba-e- Urdu) played the father of the bride groom.

According to Majaz's sister, Hamida Salim, "This period of Aligarh Muslim University can be termed the golden period. In this period, Aligarh gave birth to the stars who brightened every nook and corner of the country. In every field, be it literature, poetry, society or politics, Aligarian stars were dominantly present.

It seemed as if streams of knowledge and learning were gushing forth from here and giving a new life to the whole of the country. If someone was an enthusiastic social worker, another was a fervent and bold soldier of the freedom struggle. Every one seemed to be mad with the intention of rooting out the old system; prepared to help and co-operate with one another with heart, soul, money and might. A few of the names that occur to my memory right now are all well-known: Saadat Hasan Manto, Ali Sardar Jafri, Sibt-e-Hasan, Shahid Lateef, Akhtarul Iman, Akhtar Raipuri, Jan Nisar Akhtar, Moin Ahsan Jazbi, Khwaja

Ahmad Abbas, Majaz and Ansar Harwani. In that period, Ismat Chughtai and Safia Jan Nisar Akhtar were also active from behind the curtain. Those having literary taste were occupied to decide and solve the riddle of 'Art for Art's Sake' or 'Art for Life's Sake.' They were busy in making literature relevant to day-to-day life. This movement came to be known as progressive literature. Youths concerned with this movement included some whose tones and tenors were highly aggressive and dominating. Some supported the Partition of the country under the false impression of the ideology of 'self-determination.' However, there is no denying that each one of them had a goal before him and was fully cautious of the prevailing scenario. They were passionate to do away with the British regime and the system based on capitalism. If one used pen as a sword; another was physically active.

Zia compound is situated on the Marris Road —where Majaz, Ansar Harwani, Safia and Hamida lived and on the opposite side was that tall and clumsy wall of the Girl's Hostel behind which their dream-girls lived. Therefore, this road was quite appropriate for evening walk. Though fresh air was available on the roads of the University, but this road had something special about it. Everyone was concerned with 'for what this much distance from the close ones (beloved)?"

Hamida writes: "In that period, the position of Israr Bhai was like a candle on which thousands of moths struggled to sacrifice their lives. Between the candle and the moths was the awkward and high wall of the girls' hostel. But more stony and thorny than the wall are the values of the hour which determine the worth of a man not with his attributes of nobility but with swelling pockets with money."

Ismat Apa writes, "Girls kept hidden the photograph of their favourite poet, Majaz, in their books. Girls used to toss for his name. The wall of the hostel was possible to be made a hole through, but the social values were not to be flexible a bit. The mothers behind the wall kept on taking sighs and their candle flickered to die down bit by bit. All the girls were left dejected and empty-handed; they could not even have the last look."

Hamida Salim tells about her second brother Ansarul Haq Harwani: "The Aligarh scenario helped, to a great extent, the nationalism of Ansar Bhai which he had developed during the Khilafat Movement when the milieu was resounding with slogans of "Up with Gandhiji" and "Up with Ali Brothers," the same nationalism which had gained nourishment from the speeches of the leaders at the park of Aurangabad. During his stay in Aligarh, his nationalism flourished and developed to the fullest day-by-day.

On reaching Aligarh, Ansar Bhai was admitted to the Minto Circle School of the University. Soon, friendship developed between him and Bachhu Bhai (Khwaja Ahmad Abbas). It is also an interesting fact that red Turkish cap of cotton of Ansar Bhai became the object of mutual attraction for them because the seniors considered it to be disgraceful to befriend their juniors. At that time, Bachhu Bhai was in the university and Ansar Bhai in the school.

During the study period, having a walk on the platform of the railway station late at night was a favourite pastime of Ansarul Haq Harwani. Breaching the laws of the Proctor's office was delightful, no doubt. There were possibilities of having the chance to see the face of a beautiful girl boarding or getting down the train. In winter nights, hot tea of the station had a distinct taste of itself.

Hamida Salim says, "He was very handsome in his youth. He was fond of delicious food, attractive attire and dressing well. In this context, Achhu Bhai mentions an incident. Late night, he came to our house to take Ansar Bhai to the platform. The friends had planned to make sound of barking below the window as an indication for Ansar Bhai to come out stealthily. Once, he got late in coming out. The friends asked the reason. Ansar Bhai replied that he was searching the cold cream which was not available because of dark. The friends asked for what he was searching the cold cream? He replied, "Maybe I have a chance to see a girl luckily." He wore cotton but was very cautious of the whiteness and ironing, etc. of his Kurta and Pajama.

Youth has its own requirements. To satisfy them, he and his friends would often go to Abdullah Lodge. He was very close to Papa Mian (Shaikh Abdullah). Supporting the women's education and participating in the movement was but an excuse. That time. the building of the Lodge was equal to Heaven. Its girls were beautiful, educated and free from the limitations of veil. In the days to come, Harwani became so occupied with political and social services that Independence of the country made him forget every thing.

Ansarul Haq Harwani was also a close friend of Firoz Gandhi. When Indira Gandhi was undergoing the romantic pangs of her youth and was madly in love with Feeroz Gandhi, she remained tense because of Panditji's hesitation in showing the green light. Ansar Harwani helped Indiraji feel relaxed. Ansar Harwani published the news of the expected marriage of Indiraji with Feeroz Gandhi in his newspaper; National Herald on the morning Panditji was to reach Lucknow from Allahabad. Harwani did it on the signal from Rafi Ahmad Qidwai. Panditji was a visionary. He verified the news rather than letting the word spread far and wide and providing people an opportunity to make it a subject of discussion at tea shops. In Vardha, the betrothal ceremony of Indiraji and Feeroz Gandhi was announced under the guardianship of Gandhiji."

The Urdu writing which flourished from the campus of Aligarh Muslim University also includes with distinction the letters of Safia Jan Nisar Akhtar. Safia studied from class VIIth in the Girls' School upto the University and joined the Teachers' Training School. She was the sister of Majaz, Ansar Harwani and Hamida Salim; wife of Jan Nisar Akhtar, and mother of the famous lyricist of Bolywood, Javed Akhtar.

In 1936, she passed the examination of Intermediate with distinction from the Aligarh Girl's College. From the very beginning, Safia was popular as Majaz's sister in the college. Then the classes of B.A. were held without any screen. Some lady teachers took the classes and few classes, taken by the male teachers of the university, were held with screen. Aal-e- Ahmad Suroor has written in his autobiography, *Khawab Baqi Hain*, "On the request of Shaikh Abdullah, he had also taken some classes of Urdu with screen. Safia was bold enough to challenge the unrequited limitations and outdated social practices. According to Hamida Salim, "We both sisters remained with uncovered face in Aligarh. The year 1942 proved to be of immense help for Safia Aapa. A cousin of Salma Aapa came to Girls' College to see her. He wished to see Safia Aapa as she was the sister of his friend Majaz. He must have also heard about her from Salma Aapa. It was the first evening when Safia and Akhtar saw each other. A wandering soul, indifferent to the self, to the surroundings, soft- and slow-spoken, somewhat shameful in appearance, with some untidy locks of hair lying on the forehead, and sometimes trying to manage them with slight jolts to the neck—it was Akhtar. Who knew then that whole of his life is full of such uneasiness and complexities which he is tired of in an attempt to resolving. He is tired, no doubt, but looks forward for a hand.

"In short, Bhai Akhtar's romantic style and poetic thoughts and temperament won Safia Aapa's heart in the first meeting. Since her tastes were the same as that of Akhtar, their mutual feelings were natural. What else does a thirsty wish for, except water?"

Safia's first letter to Jan Nisar Akhtar, published in her first book of letters, namely, *Harf Aashna* is as follows:

> "Dear Akhtar,
>
> You must be surprised to see this strange writing...Anyway, the action is bold, no doubt... perhaps traditional values may be challenged by this

act of mine. But, I am helpless since I find you wherever there are chains of traditions lying shattered."

On December 25, 1943, Safia was married to Akhtar in Lucknow. After marriage, Safia lived for about nine years and passed away on January 17, 1953. Her Letters, which Jan Nisar published posthumously, under the titles of *Harf Aashna* and *Zer-e-Lab* are a considerable contribution to Urdu literature and a part of cultural history of Aligarh.

After marriage, Safia writes in the first letter to Akhtar from Aligarh, "I am O.K. How charming and dull the life is... your imagination has enlightened whole of my life...Even this feeling is precious to me...all the day, girls and teachers of the college make a noise and look at me in the hope of getting some pearls stitched on my garments. Then ignoring my carelessness and awkward dressing, they ask me, "Are you fresh?" Though this question is also not right because, unfortunately, I have lost all my freshness and charm. I don't know whether or not I will get a witness for that.

Safia loved very much her brother, Majaz. She was not only proud of her brother, she was anxious for him. Jan Nisar Akhtar and Majaz were not only friends but also the popular poets of the boys and girls of Aligarh. Both were progressive, and were known for their poetry. Both were alcoholic and were of changing moods. Salma Haqqui writes, "When Safia recited and sang Majaz's poem, full of emotions, in the hostel of the Girl's College, every one was spellbound. The poem was, *Ai gham-e-dil kya karun, ai wahshat-e-dil kya karun?* (What to do O sorrows of life, what to do O loneliness?). In love, Safia felt the pain and anguish of the brother. Whoever listened to Majaz's poems in Safia's voice, tears rolled down his cheeks. Majaz started taking wine in excess and became a great problem for Safia and the parents. Safia wrote to Jan Nisar: "There is no news of Israr Bhai. We don't know whether or not he is in Delhi. You cannot imagine his *seemabpai*....he has become unaware of all the feelings. He has only one goal for which he can indulge in any vice...The mother remains restless. Even if she wants father to go somewhere he is unable because of his handicap (he was lame). I am entirely helpless because of the child. We all have hope in you alone."

As a mother, Safia writes about the adolescence and mischiefs of Javed Akhtar, "... Thank God, Javed in jolly. Whenever he sees a beautiful girl he prepares to die for her... the responsibilities of children have checked the progress of all my plans. You have suggested that I should murder both the children and come to you. The suggestion seems to be O.K. but who will bell the cat? Javed takes the pipe in the mouth, puts on the glasses and sits in the chair to copy his uncle (Majaz)... In short, he is really an actor...I am dispatching you Jadu's two letters. His birth seems to me as if a matter of yesterday and now he has started writing letters. I feel proudly happy to see his brilliance. I have extracted the best of yours and adopted!"

She writes a letter to Janisar Akhtar about Jadu with reference to his teacher when he was studying in school, "When the teacher asked the students to sketch the India's flag, Jadu made a red flag with a hammer and sickle instead of the Tricolour. "In her letters, there are frequent references with regard to Jadu's growth as a progressive comrade. She writes very proudly that he tells his uncle's and grand father's names as Ghalib and Stalin. These letters of Safia reflect a mother's love and upbringing. Today, we witness its effects. Javed Akhtar has brought glory to his mother's name and to his self in the world of Indian cinema and literature.

Javed Akhtar, a 15 year old boy studying in Aligarh Muslim University School, wrote his first love letter, handed it over to the girl in the badminton court was followed by the song 'Ek Ladki Ko Dekha" from "1942 – A Love Story".

Safia Salim tells about her study period, "We all were eight students in M.A. (final) in economics. It is also a matter of surprise that despite so much social limitation, three of us love-married with fellows of the same department. The affairs started with the exchange of journals and books of the seminar, and not with love-letters. At last, after many years, the fellowship of class turned into fellowship of life with the good offices of Safia Aapa and Mahmood Sb. I regard it a great favour of Aligarh on me.

The author of Rivayat-e-Aligarh, Mr. Muhammad Zakir Ali Khan who established Sir Syed University of Engineering and Technology (SSUET) at Karachi in Pakistan, writes about the days of his study at Aligarh, "Every Aligarian, irrespective of his age, turns romantic on hearing the name of Marris Road and begins taking cold sighs. Forgetting his age, he is filled with youth and vitality. Name the road and like greedy Mullas, Aligarians begin dreaming of Hoors from Heaven. Unable to check their emotions, poets have written poems glorifying the Road. Not only that, poems were also written on the Lorries and Tongas plying on the road, which are lively, even today after fifty years. By 1950, this passageway of the fairies was worshipped, but now branches of this road have spread throughout the university. Before 1950, girls studying B.T., geography and science had to go to the university with faces covered. Therefore, lovers regarded following the Lorries and other vehicles more befitting than attending the class. Like all other educational institutions, there were students of every taste in Aligarh also. The best category was that of the studious boys followed by sports-enthusiasts who rushed to the play ground after classes were over. One category liked to remain in hostel and regarded it as their part of education, but there were some lovers also who did not rest until take a walk of the Marris Road. These boys would go to Marris Road in the evening, all dressed, tidy and well-groomed, and kept wandering here and there on bicycles. Back to hostel, they usually told stories, mostly fabricated.

One of my class fellows had also joined their group and had become habitual. This gentleman used to follow a particular tonga. Taking pity on him once, the girls dropped a letter from the tonga, which read, I have an urgent piece of work, please come tomorrow. Having read it, he was filled with joy. Next day, he reached with much make-up but got no response from the tonga. Two or three days, rather, a week passed which added to his misery. At last, on the seventh day, he received the apology "I had to remain silent because one of the friends had seen me dropping the paper. I will write soon when I have a chance." The fellow was patient, so kept on with them. Thus, days, weeks and months passed but the expected friend could not be traced. Nevertheless, he continued with his chase of the tonga. After much wait, he saw a silver lining. This time, a very stylish and romantic envelope was dropped from the tonga. Our friend hurriedly picked it and put in the pocket instead of kissing it and reading it. Even his friend on the bicycle could not have a glimpse of it. In solitude, when he opened the much-awaited letter with all love, it read, "O mongoose, you have wasted lots of time. Go and look at the mirror and return from where you've come." This incident was also narrated to the university students by their relative girls so that the 'mongoose' could be traced, and he becomes known with a view to alerting others of his category. Thank God, these 'mongooses' of the forties are still among us, but grey hairs have covered their faces, and now they go to Masjid five times a day in place of Marris Road. While talking, they mention Ulemas and saints of the community instead of beautiful girls. In such a scenario, I fear Allah calling them mongoose.

The Students' Union also played a key role in spreading awareness about distinguished women, and in promoting the cause of women's education. In 1926, the Union invited Annie Besant in its meeting and honoured her with the honorary life membership of the Union. In 1935, life membership was also awarded to Khalida Adeeb Khanam of Turkey. Nightingale of India, Sarojini Naidu visited AMU on numerous occasions. Mukhtar Masood says, "Once, the mother asked smilingly, 'Who is this *Kafir* (infidel) whose father was her fan when she was young and now when she is old, her son is her fan".

Mukhtar Masood describes Sarojini Naidu's visit of the 1948 in these words: "There was no room left even for a foothold in the Union and Strachey Hall. It was the first meeting of its kind. A year ago, even the imagination of welcoming a Hindu Congress leader in the university was hard. In a few months, the scenario has completely changed. Two independent countries came into existence in place of the British India. Independence proved to be expensive. There was hue and cry everywhere. There was great loss of lives and property, which turned people helpless and resourceless. Those who died remained lying and those who were alive were like living dead bodies. There was bloodshed in every part of the country but the university remained safe. Then, bad rumours began pouring. Some said preparations are on to attack on the university; attackers are being trained in the nearby villages and they will invade the university from all sides. On the university side, it was decided that children and women will be locked in the safe building of Sir Syed Hall in case of an attack and the youthful boys will fight outside. Some arrangements were also made to get the information of attack before hand. There was restlessness without doubt, but we did not have disbelief in the least. But who can harm one whom Allah saves. So Muslim University remained unharmed. There were people who guarded it and assured every security. One of them was Sarojini Naidu.

When she stood in the Strachey Hall to address, there was belief that she will announce formal and conditional security of the university. Along with Sarojini, there were some Hindus also wearing Gandhi cap, sitting in the first row. Every Gandhian was alerting Sarojini that Muslims are rivals, so they must be treated on that footing. Sarojini started her speech and on the very first sentence all were shocked. First sentence was completed and we were all surprised while those who came with her were stunned. She said, "Today, I have come here against the will of many and inspite of warning from a few. First the State Congress and then the district congress of Aligarh asked me to cancel my visit. They forgot that as a Governor, I am no more the member of congress party. Therefore, I am bound neither to their advice nor their by-laws. As for threats, I have never paid any attention to them. So, I have come. Who can stop the nightingale from going to the orchard?" On hearing this, we all thanked God. Who can put out a candle lit and guarded by angels?

After a long period of ten months, Sarojini delivered a speech. "The clouds of disbelief have shattered. Aligarh has got its now position. Now, it is also the Sarojini's Aligarh besides that of Sir Syed. Tomorrow, God knows who will claim Aligarh to be his. It's like a river, gushed forth from high mountains and is on its way to sea while benefiting the dry lands in between."

In the evening, a function was held in Sarojini's honour in the Students' Union Hall. I participated in this programme. There were intense feelings and emotions all around. This might have been the last programme in the Hall of the Union in my career of study. After some days, we'll leave the place. The father had spent twenty years of his youth (which he terms 'life achievement') in the service of the institution.

I entered the Union Hall for the first time with my mother as a student of class III and sat behind the veil in the girls' rows. That was in 1935, now it is 1948 and I have appeared in the examination of M.A. That was my first programme in the Union's Hall and today I have attended the programme as a student for the last time. That day, I could understand none, and today I have come to convince people of my points. Crowd was there that day, too, but the mother was sitting in the Hall.

Like the first meeting, in this last meeting also, the chief guest was a woman. In both of them, features are almost the same. By virtue of her gender, woman is tender; by virtue of being women, hardworking and struggling. That lady was revolutionary and progressive, this one was also. That was unmatched in writing; this, in speech. That was the nymph of *Koh-e-Qaf*; this was nightingale of India. That was known as Khalida Adeep Khanam and this is known as Sarojini Naidu. Between these meetings, I had covered the period in the University's Student's Union Hall. Today, when the programme started, we lacked a Majaz who may have penned a poem, "To Sarojini Naidu" like "To Khalida" and recited it with all fervour. However, there are many verses of Majaz that fit on Sarojini also. Majaz mentioned, in the poem for Khalida, her attributes of soft-spokenness, freedom-loving, asked her the secrets of Independence, asked for blowing the trumpet of awareness and discovered the spell in her talks.

When Sarojini stood to speak, she was welcomed with floral garlands. I have never seen a parallel to this tradition of the Union Hall. Though I saw many great welcome ceremonies in great nations, full of grandeur and splendour, but the way Union Hall welcomes has its own unique charm by virtue of being simple. In the Union Hall, right above the dice, there is a *mustatil* opening which is surrounded by inventilators. Around this ceiling inventilator, petals of carnation flower are stored in mass quantity on the roof. The chief guest stands right beneath it. When the guest comes on the stage and takes his position, there is clapping while he is silent. As soon as the clapping stops and he starts speaking, it begins raining flower petals. First in slow motion and gradually in bigger quantity. When the flower petals fall from a considerable height, the dancing petals look very charming. First they appear to be drops of rain and then there is a series of pearls from the sky to the earth. They say that light descends upon the pious; no doubt. But I have witnessed flowers raining on some good people form the sky. The scene is such that it leaves indelible marks on one's memory. And one who stands once on this stage always feels under the weight of flowers.

When petals began raining on Khalida Adeeb Khanam, she was surprised, looking above to know where the petals were falling from, but every time, the petals covered her face. She was impressed so much that she referred to it in her book which she authored after the visit of the great continent. Today, Sarojini was on the stage. The spectators also saw the new relation between flower and nightingale. The flowers were kissing her feet. When the nightingale's turn came, she said, "I have come here in the Union's Hall after a long period. It is these flowers and emotions of the youths which bridge the gap. We rained flowers on her; in response, she opened the barrage of pearls on us."

The Academic Calander of the University indicates that in 1935, Mrs. Duncan who was the Honorary Lady Teacher, and Miss Qamar Jahan Jafar Ali, who had obtained the Diploma of Montessary from London, had joined the faculty of school. Prof. Naseem Ansari had also joined the school in that very period. He writes, "Miss Qamar Jahan was the supervisor of the school. When he became a bit younger, he started taking lessons of English from the English lady, Mrs. Duncan. Boys and girls studied together.

In 1935, three ladies, namely, Begum Sir Mian Muhammad Shafi (Lahore), Begum Sahiba Sir Syed Imam Ali (Patna) and Dr. (Miss) Noor Jahan, M.A. Ph.D. Inspector of Schools (Shahjahanpur) used to participate with men as members of the supreme governing body , the University Court.

On October 8, 1933 Atiya Begum wrote to Sir Ross Masood (AMU Vice Chancellor), "Would you hold an All Asia Muslim Ladies Conference with a view of founding a Muslim Women's University in Aligarh? I shall get lady-delegates from all Eastern countries and it may even by throw open to America, Italy...."

Sir Ross Masood wrote back in reply; "I am afraid, Aligarh will not suitable, as we are not in a position in the university to make the necessary arrangements for a conference of this kind".

But till before Independence, it was mandatory for women to wear the *burqa*. Qurratul Ain Haider describes the situation of that period in these words, "Then, I arrived at Aligarh in order to do M.A. in English. By then, girl students had got permission to attend lectures in the University. However, they had to put on *burqa*. Since, I was the only girl student at MA English, the question arose whether a screen be erected in the classroom in order to segregate me. The British Professor Fielden suggested that I should sit outside the classroom, draped in *burqa*. I thought he was jocking. However, when he insisted on the same, pointing out that *burqa* was compulsory, I left Aligarh for Lucknow. My mother had given up *burqa* when she had arrived in Aligarh years ago in 1920. She had persuaded the wives of some University teachers to give up burqa. It was inconceivable for me to revert to the old practice, and that too, after the passing of a quarter of century . I said goodbye to Aligarh and set for Lucknow.

During the period, Aligarh was quite progressive and liberal and reflected a readiness to accept change. The daughter of Shaikh Abdullah, Khursheed Mirza became Renuka Devi, the heroine of Bombay Talkies in 1939, but Muslims did not withdraw their girls from the school in protest. After some years, the daughter-in-law of Shaikh Abdullah who had married Mohsin Abdullah also became the film heroine, known as Naina. Earlier, another girl from Aligarh, Zubaida Haq had joined the film industry, know as Begum Para. She was the heroine of the first Indian talkie movie, *Aalam Aara*, which is now a part of Indian film history. Khursheed Mirza worked in films like *Jeevan Parbat, Bhabhi, Naya Sansar, Sahara, Ghulami, Samrat Chandra Gupta*, etc. When her first film was released and people saw gentle Muslim girls dancing on the screen, the local newspapers made scathing attack on Shaikh Abdullah. In defence, the Sheikh argued that father was not accountable for the decisions of a married girl; the husband was.

Another alumna of Aligarh, Tahira Husain writes: "This family was highly educated and modern. Its services for the promotion of women's education in Indian sub-continent are unique. However, when his daughter Khursheed Abdullah and son Mohsin Abdullah joined the film industry along with his bride Begum Shahida, the respectable families of Aligarh withdrew their girls from the school. Even the name of my sisters were changed which were earlier, Birjees and Khursheed and they were stopped from going to school. It was a major jolt for the educational evolution of Indian women. Khursheed Abdullah worked under the name of Renuka Devi; and Shahida, Naina. Both earned much fame. *Man Ki Jeet* and *Doosari Shadi* are famous films of Naina. Later on, these people shifted to Pakistan. Khursheed Aapa became popular by the name of 'Akka Bua' on the Pakistan T.V. and worked for a long period for Pak. T.V. (In 1985, Pakistan's President, Gen. Ziaul Haq had awarded her the Presidential Award for her performance in recognition of her services in the Department of T.V. Drama.). However, Shahida took divorce from Mohsin Abdullah and married the famous film producer W.Z. Ahmad and spent rest of the life in solitude."

Tahira Husain also writes, "In our times, the famous and popular teachers included the teacher of psychology, Mrs. Zohra Verma. One of her daughters, Sarikha Verma now plays the role of mother in films. Second daughter was Parveen Murad who got the education of medicine and married the famous film star Naseeruddin Shah who is also an Aligarian. Unfortunately, the marriage could not be successful. One day, Perveen Murad was found dead on Marris Road in the biting cold of December. Besides, other well-known ladies were Shahnaz Hashmi, teacher of English and sister of Saad Hashmi, Salma Siddiqui, daughter of Rasheed Ahmad Siddiqui, who had taught us Urdu. She taught us Urdu Ghazal and was herself an embodiment of Ghazal. Since we were good in Urdu, she had included us in his Good Book. In that period, word spread far and wide regarding her separation from husband, Khursheed Muneer, and attachment with well-known progressive short story writer, Krishna Chanda. On one occasion, Israrul Haq Majaz disclosed the relation of Krishn Chand and Salma Aapa in a mood of emotions that it was he who had brought Salma and Krishna Chanda closed to each other for the first time in Delhi. And, these meetings were transformed into marriage, later on.

Dr. Begum Naseem Iqtidar, an alumna of Aligarh Muslim University and a renowned Urdu writer, while giving an account of events in 1940s writes: "Begum Suhaila Mohammad Habeeb (mother of Professor Irfan Habeeb) used to drive her car by herself. She played tennis with male players and enjoyed the post of Honorary Magistrate and used to go to the court regularly. She kept herself involved in the social work till her last breath. She also took interest in the cultural activities in the University and was often made Judge to the cultural events. Every year she hosted a high tea party for ladies only at her home. The tea party was organized with a lot of commotion and zeal with great arrangement. She always accompanied her husband in foreign journeys. Despite all this liberal activities and freedom she was never made a subject to malicious criticism in or around the University campus. There would perhaps be none who enjoyed such respect and honour as she did."

Begum Naseem Iqtidar Ali while describing her student life writes that "we used to go to Girls' College fully clad in *Burqa* and was usually accompanied by three or four girls in one rickshaw. We took special caution that the rickshaw does not pass through the road in front of Sir Syed Hall. It is embarrassing now to tell the reason. Boys used to sit by their windows and performed a one sided oration. It still makes me laugh when I remember the sober and humorous comments. A film '*Aan*', starring Dilip Kumar, was released those days which was very popular. A song of that film '*hum aaj apni maut ka samaan le chale*' received tremendous popularity. Boys often used to follow the girls' rickshaws on their bicycles singing this song."

After Independence, the scenario of women's education changed not only in India but also there came many changes in the educational, literary and cultural activities of Aligarh. Women's College had, by now, become fully a part of the university and the prospects of women's education were quite bright. After Independence, the University earned a name for its cultural activities. Boys and girls took parts together in dramas. In youth festivals also, boys and girls presented their programmes together. They attended *Mushairas* and literary sittings together.

On the cultural activities of the university after 1947, Prof. Athar Siddiqui who himself was its student in 1947, writes in his autobiography, *Mein Kya Meri Hayat Kya.* "We had only one girl class fellow, Mustafa Bano Zuberi. She was a good friend of mine and I would go to teach her zoology at her home." He makes mention of two girls at the standard Xth, Safia Bi and Shaukat Bi. While mentioning them, he could not help expressing his fondness, "Within one year, I had developed a spot for Safia in my heart and I enjoyed the time, spent with them. On the other hand, Safia, too, liked me but thanks to the values prevailing in Aligarh in those days, we could not disclose our feelings, nor was there any question of it. Only eyes communicated with each other, lips were helpless. I had grown so fond of Safia that I composed verse for her though I was not a poet. I still remember the verse." They decided to send Safia to Pakistan for the rest of her studies. While parting I could not say anything to Safia save a humble gift, which I gave to her while she gave me a handkerchief embroidered by her. But, all these things happened at the time of her departure. We could not even get time to extract any meaning out of this exchange nor could we exchange a few words as Safia Bi had been married in 1954, but I was still a bachelor. I did see two or three girls but they did not appeal to me."

Prof. Athar Siddiqui sheds light on this changing scenario of Aligarh Muslim University, "In Irshad Manzil, where Mohsin Qureshi lived with Usman (Adhami), some lady teachers of the Women's College, including Kaniz Fatima, Masooda and Abida Shakoor used to come daily in the evening to play badminton. In neighbourhood, some women like Surayya Sultana, etc. had also become members of the club. At this spot only, Usman met Masooda for the first time and he fell in love with her. Soon, his love became intense...so much so that he did not like to see any other girl or to talk about any one else.

One of Usman's sisters, Zakia, was a student of B.A. in Women's College. One day, Usman went there to see his sister and by chance I, too, had gone there to see some one. At exact the same time, Zakia came out of Sultani Hostel to see her brother before the Provost's office.

Usman introduced me to her and told her that I was his friend and worked in the same department. We exchanged greetings. I still remember the scene of meeting Zakia. On July, 15, 1956, we both were married. Zakia Adhami now had become Zakia Ather Siddiqui. Prof. Zakia Ather Siddiqui has been the Principal of Women's College for a long period.

Qurratul Ain Haider writes about these days, "In 1956, when I went to Aligarh for some days, I saw a girl riding on a bicycle coming to see my cousin Zohra Aapa. She was another cousin of mine who had come to see me. I felt happy that now girls are free and riding on the bicycle. Furthermore, I felt pleasure when a dance teacher came and started to instruct the small child of my cousin the Kathak dance. Head of the Department of English, Mahmood Saheb's daughter, Anwari, had gone to Shanti Niketan to learn Kathakali. It's surprising that Aligarh has completely changed."

By 1950, girls used to see and hear the proceedings of the Strachey Hall and Union Hall of the University from galleries upstairs. But during the Vice-Chancellorship of Dr. Zakir Husain Saheb, Zohra Naqvi, student of M.Sc (Physics) was the first to be elected the member of the Cabinet of the Student's Union.

Zohra also went to America for higher studies and became the space scientist. Thus, in 1906, whereas girls were brought to schools in the sedans, now scientist like Zohra Naqvi was flying in the space. According to Dr. Abdullah, Abdullah of US, "When I joined Aligarh, mostly girls were clad in *burqa*, few were without *burqa*. But with the passage of time, the ratio had completely changed."

In 1955-56, I carried a tour of the students of M.Sc. (Zoology) to Madras and Mandapam. It was also a good, now and strange experience. The group consisted of both, boys as well girls."

In the 1958-Academic Session of the University, the total number of boys and girls were 4 thousand and 774. Of them, girls studying in the Women's College were 254; and those studying in Girls' High School were 465. The result of this school was 94 per cent, while that of S.T. High School was 83 per cent. In 1958 itself, the name of women's Hall was changed to Abdullah Hall. Arrangements for sports had also been made for girls. From 18-20 December, 1957, Women's College also celebrated its Jubilee function in which Old Girls from India and abroad participated in great numbers. On this occasion, arrangements were also made for Art Exhibition, which about 2,000 people saw. Same year, the Principal of Women's College, Prof. Mrs. Mumtaz Jahan Haider went to Britain and America as a representative of the Indian government to study the educational system of universities there. In her absence, Miss Joseph acted as the Principal.

By 1960, the Aligarh girls were also getting traditional education like other Indian girls. But after the establishment of Jawaharlal Nehru Medical College in 1962, girls were attracted towards medical education and in 1966 when women's Polytechnic was established, girls turned towards vocational education. At Womens' Polytechnic, where Diploma Course like costume designing and secretarial practice are offered, girls are getting technical and professional education of Electronics, Engineering, Computer Engineering and Information Technology, etc.

The General Education Centre is playing a key role in the promotion of cultural and literary activities of the students besides teaching and research. It is noticeable that when the national anthem or the University Tarana is sung in University functions the girls stand in the front and the boys behind them. Kennedy Hall is now the Centre of such activities where Drama Club, Music Club, Film Club and Literary Club are housed.

As a Visiting Professor in 1980, noted fiction writer, Qurratul Ain Haider observed a marked change in Aligarh ethos. Girls freely interacted with boys in staging plays and rode cycles. They joined boys in chorus songs. As part of a cultural programme, the University *tarana* was presented on stage, with the girls standing in the front and the boys at the back. The University *tarana* which is composed by Majaz, stirred everyone's heart, as it was sung with the accompanying orchestra. The daughter of Dr. Nasim Ansari and Dr. Zinat Ansari was the captain of University Horse Riding Club. Girls fared better than boys in the entire competitive field. Yet the stereotype of a hapless, victimized *burqa*-clad Muslim woman persists. Indian press has clung all along to this stereotypical image. Over the years I have been subject to this consistent, though tormenting, remark: Oh! How enlightened and modern you are! You are not at all like a typical Muslim woman."

In the University, girls' education has become common in due course of time and women have been scaling new heights. If we take a view of the results of the tenth class of schools affiliated to the university, like City High School, Saifuddin Tahir High School and Girls' High School, we come to know that result of Girls' High School was the best, i.e., 95 per cent, then S.T. High School with 76 per cent followed by the City High School with just 41 per cent. Then, there were seven faculties in the University. Except the faculty of law, there was not a single faculty in which girls were not studying. In some cases, girls outnumbered boys. For instance, in B.A. (1st-year), there were 73 boys and 87 girls. In M.Ed. both were equal. In the faculty of Arts, the total number of students was 1,262. Of them, boys were 749 and girls 513. In the faculty of science, the total number of students was 2,019 with 1,780 boys and 239 girls. In B.Sc. (Engineering) also, there were four girls while one girl was studying in M.Sc. (Engineering). There pretty many girls in M.B.B.S. as compared to B.U.M.S. There were 226 enrolments in M.B.B.S., of them, 167 boys and 59 girls. In B.U.M.S., the total was 197, i.e., 187 boys and 10 girls. In the faculty of Theology, the total was 8, i.e., 2 boys and 6 girls. In short, total students at the university level were 5 thousand and 961. Of them, 835 were girls.

In the rifle shooting contest, Miss Iffat Ara Zaidi was awarded the Vice-Chancellor Prize. Similarly, in the field of sports, girls were taking part. There used to be a full-fledged, women's visiting committee to review the tasks of cleanliness of the hostels and to help provosts in maintaining discipline in the kitchen and the Dining Hall. Four women had been entrusted the task to see the arrangements of the hostels. Mrs. Ziauddin Ansari was its President. Other members were Begum J.P. Singhal, Begum Jamal Khwaja, and Mrs. Zohra Verma. D.S.W. looked after the arrangements of the Secretary and convenor.

In 1972, when I was admitted in the Pre-University, literary and cultural activities marked the atmosphere of the entire campus in the university. In the evening, playgrounds were also full of boys and students were engaged in games of their choice. Scholarly discussions were held on *Café de Laila and Café de Phoos*. Preparations for the annual celebrations of the hostels began much earlier. Students were provided every opportunity to strengthen their personality. I used to take part in *Baitbazi*, on behalf of N.R.S.C. and during my period of study, I remembered thousands of verses. But the game was won by the girls, because they had more verses in their memory than boys.

Girls were not allowed to go to Boys' Hostel in general, but during the Hall's celebrations, the girls always took part in the contests of the Halls. Rihana Khusro who is presently the teacher of Fine Arts was an enchanting singer in that period. Many girls recited ghazals.

As the professional education became common among girls, the university administration also paid special heed towards it. In 1970, there was only one hostel for girls — Abdullah Hall.

Later on, a Hall of residence was constructed after the name of Sarojini Naidu where students of M.B.B.S., Engineering, Diploma Engineering and Post Graduation were allotted room. When this Hall also became insufficient, a new Hall for girls was constructed after the name of Indira Gandhi in 1994, near Kankar wali Kothi, Lal Diggi Road during the Vice-Chancellorship of Professor Muhammad Naseem Farooqui. And now, the fourth girl's hostel named Sultan Jahan Hall after the name of its first Chancellor, has come up.

Before this, during the Vice-Chancellorship of Syed Hamid Sb, the issue of nurses in the Medical College Hospital had turned serious. Many nurses of the J.N. Medical College began going to Arab countries for jobs. So, a school of nursing was started formally on the campus of the Medical College where a three-year diploma of general nursing and midwifery is given and these diploma holder nurses are placed in the Medical College. Before 1982, there was not a single Muslim nurse. The majority was of the Christian nurses from Kerala, but now that scenario has changed.

In 1978-79, when I took admission to the B.Ed. course, it seemed as if the class was being held in Women's College instead of the university. The percentage of girls in B.Ed. was 70 and the teachers were mostly ladies, including Safia Aapa, Prof. Ghazala Ansari, Mrs. Awais and Prof. Sajida Zaidi. Prof. Sajida Zaidi would light the cigarette before entering the classroom and start teaching after smoking for a few seconds. Her younger sister, Prof. Zahida Zaidi taught us English in B.A. She, too, like her sister kept a packet of cigarettes in her hand. In those days, Zaidi sisters were looked upon as Progressive ladies. Her elder sister, Sabra Zaidi, had also been the teacher in the Dept. of Education. During M.Ed also, the ratio of the boys and girls was almost the same.

In my student days, girls had started taking part in sports, too. One of my class fellows, Yasmeen Zaidi, who was the daughter of well-known Urdu writer, Ali Jawwad Zaidi, used to ride horses daily. Later on, Prof. Naseem Ansari's daughter, Zoya Ansari, had also become the captain of the riding club. Both the daughters of Wasey Usmani, teacher of the Mechanical Engineering, also did horse-riding. India Today published their photographs, riding horses on its cover page as a sign of modern women's empowerment. Saba Naheed, daughter of Khalida Madam, teacher of the Minto Circle, was an active member of the Drama Club.

In the 1983-84 academic sessions, total boys and girls in the university were 10 thousand and 588. Of them, boys were 8723 while the girls were 1865. At that time, total students in schools maintained by the university were 5783. The enrolment of A.M.U. Girls' High School was 1,659. Total departments in the University were 57. Seven departments of them had Lady Heads. The same year, the U.G.C. sanctioned a grant of 69,72,500 rupees for the construction of a hostel accommodating 200 girls in Abdullah Hall. Mrs. Shila Kaul had also attended a function of Women's College as the Minister of Education of State. Her husband was the former student of Aligarh Muslim University.

In September 1984, when I joined the Office of Public Relations of the University, the Registrar Office was in the S.S. Hall. The office of the Vice-Chancellor was where there is the Provost Office today near Victoria Gate. There was not a single woman employee in the Registrar Office, Finance Office and other offices, but today there is not a single section of the Registrar Office where there is not a woman employee.

As for the Women's College, the number of girls has been increasing at a very fast speed. New courses have been introduced. Till recently, the college offered only the graduation programme, but for some years, M.Sc. (Home Science) has also been introduced. Since 1984, career planning centre has also been offering short-term professional courses for girls in the Girls' College. Presently, girls from 14 foreign countries have been studying in different courses. On the campus of the college, there is also Sr. Sec. School (Girls), Girls' High School, Abdullah Nursery and Primary School.

As per the annual report of 2002-03, the total strength of the students at the university level was 18,580. Of them, 12 thousand 579 were boys and more than 6 thousand were girls. Students of the maintained schools are not included in it. Among the rank holders of the university, 48 are girls. It indicates that girls are outperforming boys and the ratio of students passing with distinction is also greater on the part of girls.

The former Principal of Women's College, Prof. Zakia Athar Siddiqui made efforts in 2001 to establish the women's study centre and she succeeded. The centre is part of the Faculty of Social Science. A Programme of study for women has also been introduced at the graduation level. Seventy-two such centres have been established in different universities with the aid of the U.G.C. throughout India.

According to the university annual report of the year 2004-05, there were a total of 27 thousand and 273 students both boys and girls — including the schools affiliated to the university. Thus, the ratio of girls was more than 35 per cent. Deans of four faculties out of twelve were women. They were Prof. Azarmi Dukht Safavi, Dean, faculty of Arts, and Prof. Qamer Akhtar Kazmi, Dean, faculty of Unani Medicine while the Dean of the faculty of Medicine was Prof. Shameen Jahan Rizvi. On the other hand, there was not a single woman Dean in the University of Delhi in the same year.

The distinguishing feature and remarkable thing about the university is its style of functioning. Here, the way girls are educated and trained is neither bound to old and traditional values, nor does it allow unbridled freedom. They are educated in an atmosphere which conforms to the established and acceptable values of the time so that they may differentiate between the old and new systems and may live with them. In the light of the statistics of the past fifty years, it can be predicted that the number of girls will be more than that of boys by 2015. In 2020, when the university celebrates its 100-year anniversary, the women's movement is expected to have reached its summit. The demand for a women's university is also made by the Aligarian community.

On the basis of my attachment with the university for a period spanning over thirty-three years, I can say with firm belief that except for one or two incidents, the atmosphere of the university has always been praiseworthy and free from any pollution. The only exception is that a student of the Dept. of journalism, who tried not only to defame the institution but also made a despicable effort to tell the outside world that girls are forced to live a life full of limitations. Furthermore, dress code is fully imposed on girls so that Aligarh may form a bond with the medieval times. She did all this to satisfy her petty interest. The day, she chose for her heinous drama, was by chance a memorable day in the history of women's education in Aligarh. On this day, February 2, Founder's Day, day of Women's College is celebrated with all grandeur. The girl tried to bring infamy to the university intentionally instead of paying tribute to Shaikh Abdullah (Papa Mian).

A similar case is related to a student (girl) of the Dept. of law. She used to indulge in activities like uploading articles on the Internet or sending them to English magazines in order to demean the status of the university. She had links with an organisation based in America.

In this connection, I quote the retired Professor of Chemistry, Fasih Ahmad Siddiqui: "Respect of girls is not only a part of the religion of the boys of Aligarh, but also the quintessence. They can never tolerate any activity of low grade. I claim that during the past 45 years, I have never heard a boy hurling a degrading comment on any girl anywhere on the campus, be it road, library, cafeteria, classroom and so on. Once in the class of

Biochemistry, three-fourths were girls. One day, all of them were present from the period first. It began raining and did not seem to stop the sunset. The water stood on the road up to knees. However, the girls kept entertaining themselves with no trace of anxiety on their faces. Rather, they seemed to be as comfortable as if they were in their houses. The night also began falling. The water level also decreased. Now, the boys swung into action and brought men-pulled rickshaws for girls. They rode on bicycles in twos and followed the rickshaws to the hostel or their residence. On the third day, parents of the girls came to the Department to say thanks.

I, too, have experience in some universities. If ever any girl dares pass by the boys' hostel, boys begin hurling such a language that forces one to put hands on the ears. Once, my honourable teacher, Prof. R. P. Rastogi came for the viva examination of the Ph.D. He had also to deliver a lecture. After the lecture, there was refreshment arranged by the students of M.Sc. The Professor was stunned to see the exemplary discipline on this occasion. The non-pulsed professor was the Vice-Chancellor of the Banaras Hindu University. He was a prominent Indian scientist and belonged to Lucknow. He said that Muslim culture and civilization is really great. He said, "Mostly, students of upper class come to Aligarh but their nobility is unmatched." Every one was glad to hear him. I said only that there is probably no university except Aligarh for girls in terms of safety and piety or (moral values), be it Oxford, Cambridge or Harvard. Rastogi Sb confirmed my view."

A century ago, girls of this institution faced many threats. But, today there is hardly any sphere of life where girls of Aligarh are not seen. Today, AMU girls include doctors, engineers, lawyers, writers, journalists, scientists and professors in different universities in a large number.

In the field of literature, founder of the Progressive Writers' Association, Dr. Rasheed Jahan; prominent novelist, Ismat

Chughtai, Tasneem Saleem, Chhitari; well-know writer Kusum Ansal; Safia Jan Nisar; Salma Siddiqui are to name a few. As for Electronic media, Manjari Mishra and Kalpana Jain (Times of India); Rana Afroz Siddiqui (The Hindu); Salma Zaidi (BBC); Aarfa Khanam (NDTV); Romana Khan (Sahara Samey); Poonam Sharma (Aaj Tak), Khadija Azeem; Nazish Husaini; Prabha Gupta; Saba Zaidi; Sandhia Jalal; Shahida Basu and Tahira Niyazi are worth-mentioning.

In the world of cinema, the heroine of the first speaking movie "Alam Aara" Begum Para; Renuka Devi; Naina; Sarikha Seekri Raigay; Nigar Sultana and Tabassum are well-known names. *Malika-e-Jazbat*, Nayyer Sultana, who has worked in more than 250 films in Pakistan, also belonged to Aligarh.

Similarly, in the sphere of education, Kiran Datar of the Miranda College; Professor Farah Nizami of Oxford University; Prof. Feeroza Ahmad of Princetion University, America; Prof. Yasmin Sikia of the Medicine University America; the first Muslim F.N.A in India, Prof. Qamar Rehmani; Prof. Zohra Naqvi, the space scientist, America; Prof. Zoya Hasan of Jawaharlal Nehru University and a member of National Minorities Commission , Mrs. Salma Ansari, wife of the present Vice President of India, Mr. M. Hamid Ansari, Prof. Anwar Jahan Zuberi,Vice Chancellor, Calicut University, Kerala, Prof. Hamida Ahmad, member of the University Grants Commission and Yasmeen Jalal Beg, Finance Officer of AMU are to mention a few.

Last but not least, there are women also active in politics as well as social service. Mohsina Qidwai (former Union Minister); Anwara Taimur (former Chief Minister of Assam); Abida Ahamd (former M.P. and wife of the former President of India, Fakhruddin Ali Ahmad). These women also received their education from Aligarh Muslim University.

References

1. K.A.Nizami: secular Traditions at AMU published by Public Relations Office, AMU Reference
2. Institute Gazett: 30 March, 1886.

3. Addresses and Speeches, M.A.O. College, 1875-1919, p-152, Abul Hasan).

4. Institute Gazette, Aligarh 15 May, 1912.

5. Begum Khadev Jang: An-Nazir, July 1911, P-45-46, Talimi Idara, Khuda Bakhsh Library, Patna.

6. Shaikh Muhammad Abdullah: Sawanih Umri Abdullah Begum, Aligarh.

7. Ibid p-22

8. Ibid p-23.

9. Farah Nizami: Zanana Normal School Se Muslim Girls Degree College Tak, P-158-59, "Khawateen Number" of Aligarh Magazine-2001.

10. Prof. Asghar Abbas: Sir Syed Tahreek Ki Nisai Jahat p-30.

11. Begum Sajida Zubair: Women's College ka Pas-e-Manzar, p-679. Aligarh Mera Chaman, Babul Ilm Publication, Bhopal-2001.

12. Tariq Hasan: Aligharh Movement, Rupa Publication.

13. Dr. Abida Samiuddin: Hindustan ki Jange-e-Azadi mein Muslim Khawateen ka Hissa, p-161-62.

14. Begum Sajida Zubair: Women's College ka Pas-e-Manzar, p-679. Idara Tahquiqat-e-Urdu, Patna, 1990.

15. Ismat Chughtai: Kaghzi Hai Pairahan, p-148-49.

16. Prof. Shan Muhammad: Glimpses of Muslim Education in India, p-3; Anmol Publications, Pvt. Ltd. New Delhi, 2006.

17. Aligarh Muslim University Calendar: 1932.

18. Ibid, p-23

19. Qurratul Ain Haider: Shahrah-e-Hareer, p-280; Educational Publishing House, Delhi.

20. Ali Sardar Jafri: Pather ke Shigaf, p-121. Yadein Number Aftab Hall Magazine, A.M.U. 1976

21. Hamida Akhtar Husain: Hamsafar, pp-36-37, Maktaba Daniyal, Abdulla Haroon Road, Karachi.
22. Hamida Salim: Ham Sath They: Anjuman Taraqqui Urdu (Hind) New Delhi-1991.
23. Dr. Jamal Husain Qadri: Safia Akhtar ka Aligarh, Sir Syed Day Magazine, 2002; North California, USA.
24. The Hindu, Friday July 18,2008
25. Zakir Ali Khan: Rahguzar-e-Firdaus, Sir Syed Day Magazine 2001, North California, USA.
26. Mukhtar Masood: Aawaz-e-Dost, p-181-93 Hassami Book Depot, Machhli Kaman, Hyderabad-1987.
27. Prof. Naseem Ansari: Zad-e-Rah, p-45, Mahnama Tahzeeb, Karachi — December 2004, vol-21, No:12.
28. Aligarh Muslim University Calendar: 1935
29. Ishrat Ali Qureshi: Past and Present, published by the Public Relations Office, AMU, Aligarh
30. Qurratul Ain Haider: Shahrah-e-Harier, Educational Publishing House, Delhi.
31. Lubna Kazim: A Woman of Substance, p-138, Zaban Haus Khas, New Delhi.
32. Tahira Husain: Nazr-e-Aligarh, Sir Syed Day Magazine, 2002, America.
33. Begum Nasim Iqidar Ali (mnuscript)
34. Ather Siddiqui: Main Kya Meri Hayat Kya, p-96-97, Educational Book House, Aligarh- 2003.
35. Qurratul Ain Haider, Shahrah-e-Harier, p-165.
36. Dr. Abdullah: Kuchh Yadein, Kuchh Batein, Sir Syed Day Magazine — 2002.
37. Prof. Athar Siddiqui: Mein Kya Meri Hayat Kya, p-89.
38. Annual Report....1958, Aligarh Muslim University.
39. Qurratul Ain Haider: Shahrah-e- Hairer

40. Annual Report 1966-67, Aligarh Muslim University.
41. Annual 1983-84, Aligarh Muslim University.
42. Annual 2002-03, Aligarh Muslim University.
43. Annual 2004-05, Aligarh Muslim University.
44. Prof. Fasih Ahmad Siddiqui: "Yadein Sir Syed Aur Unke Aligarh Ki." Sir Syed Day Magazine, USA.

Bibliography

Abdul Rashid Khan: *The All India Muslim Educational Conference: Its Contribution to the Cultural Development of Indian Muslims 1886-1947*, OUP, 2001.

Afkhami, M.: *Faith and Freedom: Women's Human Rights in the Muslim World*, Syracuse University Press, New York, 1995.

Alya Baffoun: *Women and Social Change in the Muslim Arab World*, Pergamon Press, 1982.

Archna Chaturvedi: *Muslim Women and Development*, Commonwealth, New Delhi, 2004.

——————: *Muslim Women and Society*, Commonwealth, New Delhi, 2004.

——————: *Muslim Women from Tradition to Modernity*, Commonwealth, New Delhi, 2004.

——————: *Muslim Women in Global Perspectives*, Commonwealth, New Delhi, 2004.

Berkey, Jonathan: *The Transmission of Knowledge in Medieval Cairo: A Social History of Islamic Education*, Princeton University Press, Princeton, 1992.

Bernadette Andrea: *Women and Islam in Early Modern English Literature*, Cambridge University Press, 2008.

Chamberlain, Michael: *Knowledge and Social Practice in Medieval Damascus, 1190–1350*, Cambridge University Press, Cambridge, 1994.

Erik C. Owens, John David Carlson, and Eric P. Elshtain: *Religion and the Death Penalty: A Call for Reckoning,* Wm. B. Eerdmans Publishing, 2004.

Fahimuddin: *Modernization of Muslim Education in India,* Adhyayan, New Delhi, 2004.

Ferree, Myra Marx: *Organizing, and Human Rights: Transnational Women's Activism*, NYU Press, 2006.

Friedmann, Yohanan: *Tolerance and Coercion in Islam: Interfaith Relations in the Muslim Tradition,* Cambridge University Press, New York, 2003.

Gaur, R.C.: *Painted Grey Ware: Proceedings of Seminar on Archaeology held at the Aligarh Muslim University*, Publication Scheme, Aligarh, 1994.

——————: *Selected Art Pieces of Aligarh Archaeological Museum,* Publication Scheme, New Delhi, 1999.

Gavin Hambly: *Women in the Medieval Islamic World*, Palgrave Macmillan, New York, 1999.

Haddad, Yvonne Y. and John L. Esposito: *Islam, Gender and Social Change,* Oxford University Press, Oxford, 1998.

Hajira Kumar: *Status of Muslim Women in India,* Aakar Books, 2002.

Hessini, L.: *Reconstructing Gender in the Middle East: Tradition, Identity & Power*, Columbia University Press, New York, 1994.

Howland, Courtney, W.: *Religious Fundamentalism and the Human Rights of Women,* St. Martins Press, New York, 1999.

Iqbal Mullick: *Rights of Muslim Women,* Cyber Tech Publications, New Delhi, 2011.

Israr Ahmed: *Religious Obligations of Muslim Women,* Adam Books, New Delhi, 2009.

Jagbir Singh: *The Jat Rulers of Upper Doab: Three Centuries of Aligarh Jat Nobility,* Aavishkar Pub, New Delhi, 2002.

Jain, M.S.: *The Aligarh Movement,* Icon, New Delhi, 2006.

Javed Ahmed Ghamidi: *Mizan,* Al-Mawrid, New Delhi, 2001.

Jean-Marie and Rehana Lafont: *The French and Delhi: Agra, Aligarh and Sardhana,* India Research Press, New Delhi, 2010.

Juhi Gupta: *The Future of Indian Muslim Women-Fatwa Versus Feminism,* Readworthy Publications, 2012.

Leila Ahmed: *Women and Gender in Islam: Historical Roots of a Modern Debate*, Yale University Press, 1992.

Levy, Reuben: *The Social Structure of Islam,* Cambridge University Press, UK, 1969.

Makdisi, George: *The Rise of Colleges: Institutions of Learning in Islam and the West,* Edinburgh University Press, Edinburgh, 1981.

Mareike Jule Winkelmann: *Reaching the Minds of Young Muslim Women: Girls' Madrasas in India,* Hope India Publications, New Delhi, 2007.

Mariam Allana: *Muslim Women and Islamic Tradition: Studies in Modernisation,* Kanishka, New Delhi, 2000.

Marín, Manuela and Randi Deguilhem: *Writing the Feminine: Women in Arab Sources,* Tauris, London, 2002.

Marmura, M.E.: *Essays on Islamic Philosophy and Science,* State University of New York Press, Albany, 1975.

Mohammad Alamgeer: *Impact of Modernism on Contemporary Muslim Women,* Axis Publications, New Delhi, 2011.

Moinuddin, S.A.H.: *Divorce and Muslim Women,* Rawat, New Delhi, 2000.

Morin, Karen, M.: *Global Perspectives on Gender and Faith,* Syracuse University Press, 2007.

Mufti Samiya Tabasum: *Status of Muslim Women in India: Law Relating to Marriage Divorce and Maintenance,* Regal Publications, New Delhi, 2013.

Naseef, Omar: *Liberation Theology: Islam and the Feminist Agenda in the Qur'an*, AuthorHouse, New Delhi, 2007.

Naseem Ahmad: *Liberation of Muslim Women*, Kalpaz, New Delhi, 2001.

Neera Bharihoke: *Rights of Hindu and Muslim Women*, Serials Pub, New Delhi, 2008.

Nonie Darwish: *Cruel and Usual Punishment: The Terrifying Global Implications of Islamic Law*, Thomas Nelson, Boston, 2008.

Pedersen, Johannes: *The Arabic Book: Translated by Geoffrey French*, Princeton University Press, Princeton, 1984.

Pietro Corsi and Paul Weindling: *Information Sources in the History of Science and Medicine*, Butterworth Scientific, London and Boston, 1983.

Qureshi, Iqbal:, *Women and Islam*, Saurabh Publishing House, New Delhi, 2007

Rahat Abrar and M. Qamar Ishaque: *Directory of Muslim Educational Institutions in India*, Institute of Objective Studies, 2002.

Rapoport, Yossef: *Marriage, Money and Divorce in Medieval Islamic Society*, Cambridge University Press, Cambridge, 2007.

Rasool, Kay: *My Journey Behind the Veil: Conversations with Muslim Women*, Lothian Books, London, 2003.

Rizzo, Helen Mary: *Islam, Democracy and the Status of Women*, Routledge, 2004.

Roded, Ruth: *Women in Islamic Biographical Collections: from Ibn Saad to who's*, Lynne Rienner Publishers, 1994.

Rosenthal, Franz: *The Technique and Approach of Muslim Scholarship*, Pontificium Institutum Biblicum, Rome, 1947.

Saadawi Nawal: *The Hidden Face of Eve*, Zed Press, London, 1980.

Sabbah, Fatna, A.: *Women in the Muslim Unconscious*, Pergamon Press, New York, 1984.

Saukath Azim: *Muslim Women: Emerging Identity,* Rawat, New Delhi, 1997.

Sedghi, Hamideh: *Women and Politics in Iran: Veiling,* Cambridge University Press, Cambridge, 2007.

Sekh Rahim Mondal: *Rural Muslim Women Role and Status,* Northern Book Centre, New Delhi, 2010.

Shaheen Akhtar and Moushumi Bhowmik: *Women in Concert: An Anthology of Bengali Muslim Women's Writings,* Stree, New Delhi, 2008.

Shalaby, Ahmad: *History of Muslim Education,* Dar al-Kashshaf, Beirut, 1954.

Shan Mohammad: *Glimpses of Muslim Education in India: Peeping Through the Convocation Addresses of The Aligarh Muslim University,* Anmol, New Delhi, 2006.

——————: *Education and Politics,* APH, New Delhi, 2002.

——————: *The All-India Muslim Educational Conference,* Select Presidential Addresses, APH, New Delhi, 2003.

Siohbhan Lambert-Hurley: *Muslim Women: Reform and Princely Patronage, Nawab Sultan Jahan Begam of Bopal,* Manohar, New Delhi, 2007.

Smith, Jane, I. and Harvard University: *Center for the Study of World Religions,* Bucknell University Press, Lewisburg PA, 1980.

Souaiaia, Ahmed, E.: *Contesting Justice: Women, Islam, Law, and Society,* State University of New York Press, 2008.

Stowassar, Barbara: *Women in the Qur'an: Tradition and Interpretation,* Oxford University Press, New York, 1994.

Suad Joseph and Afsaneh Najmabadi: *Encyclopedia of Women & Islamic Cultures,* BRILL, London, 2005.

Suad, Joseph: *Encyclopedia of Women and Islamic Cultures,* Brill Academic Publishers, London, 2008.

Syed Karamat Ali: *Perceptions and Aspirations of Industrial Workers: A Sociological Analysis of the Workers of Aligarh Lock Industry*, Uppal, New Delhi, 2007.

Syed, Mohammad Ali: *Position of Women in Islam*, State University of New York Press, New York, 2004.

Thahira M. Banu and J. Fredrick: *Work Participation of Muslim Women*, Vista International Publishing House, New Delhi, 2012.

Usha Nayar: *Education of Muslim Women and Girls in India*, The Women Press, 2011.

Van Nieuwkerk, Karin: *Women Embracing Islam: Gender and Conversion in the West*, University of Texas Press, 2006.

Wadud, Amina: *Qur'an and Woman: Rereading the Sacred Text from a Woman's Perspective*, Oxford University Press, New York, 1999.

Yamani, Mai: *Feminism and Islam, Legal and Literary Perspectives*, New York University Press, New York, 1996.

Yoginder S. Sikand: *Muslim Education in Contemporary India*, Hope India Pub, 2007.

Yvonne Haddad and John Esposito: *Islam, Gender and Social Change*, Oxford University Press, New York, 1988.

Yvonne Yazbeck Haddad, Kathleen M. Moore, and Jane I Smith: *Muslim Women in America: The Challenge of Islamic Identity Today*, Oxford University Press, New York, 2006.

Zakia, A. S.: *Muslim Women: Problems and Prospects*, Oxford, New York, 1993.

Zoya Hasan and Ritu Menon: *In a Minority: Essays on Muslim Women in India*, OUP, New Delhi, 2005.

——————: *Unequal Citizens: A Study of Muslim Women in India*, OUP, New Delhi, 2006.

Index

G

H

I

L

M

N

P

S

T

U

W

□□□